SOUTH AMERICAN AND LATIN AMERICAN ECONOMIC HISTORY

Edited by
Stuart Bruchey
Columbia University

Editorial Consultant
Herbert S. Klein
Columbia University

A GARLAND SERIES

INFLATION, GROWTH AND THE REAL EXCHANGE RATE

Essays on Economic History in Brazil and Latin America, 1850–1983

Eliana A. Cardoso

GARLAND PUBLISHING, INC.
New York and London   1987

Copyright © 1987 by Eliana A. Cardoso
All rights reserved

Library of Congress Cataloging-in-Publication Data
Cardoso, Eliana A.
  Inflation, growth and the real exchange rate.

  (South American and Latin American economic history)
  Thesis (Ph.D)—Massachusetts Institute of
Technology, 1979.
  Includes bibliographical references.
  1. Brazil—Economic policy.   2. Coffee trade—
Government policy—Brazil—History.   3. Agricultural
price supports—Brazil—History.   4. Monetary policy—
Brazil—History.   5. Foreign exchange—Brazil—History.
6. Inflation (Finance)—Brazil—History.   7. Brazil—
Commercial policy—History.   8. Economic stabilization—
I. Title.   II. Series.
  HC187.C218 1987   330.981   87-8570
  ISBN 0-8240-1356-5

All volumes in this series are printed on acid-free,
250 year-life paper.

Printed in the United States of America

INFLATION , GROWTH AND THE REAL EXCHANGE RATE :

ESSAYS ON ECONOMIC HISTORY IN BRAZIL AND LATIN AMERICA

ELIANA A. CARDOSO

Submitted in partial fulfillment
of the requirements for the
degree of

Doctor of Philosophy

at the

Massachusetts Institute of Technology
February 1979

Revised October 1985

To Serginho

ACKNOWLEDGMENTS

I am indebted to Edmar Bacha, Rudi Dornbusch and Lance Taylor, who gave me not just their comments and suggestions, but time and concern too. With all my thanks.

I wish to aknowledge financial support for my studies at MIT from CAPES, and a research grant from the Ford Foundation.

TABLE OF CONTENTS

Introduction... 1

PART I   : Essays on Economic History in Brazil :

Chapter I   :
    Exchange Rates in Nineteenth-Century Brazil........ 7
Chapter II :
    The Great Depression and the Brazilian
    Coffe-support Policy............................... 17
Chapter III :
    The Postwar Years.................................. 29
Chapter IV :
    Minidevaluations and Indexed Wages :
    The Brazilian Experience in the Seventies.......... 41

PART II   : Stabilization Experience in Latin America :

Chapter V   :
    Stabilization in Latin America :
    Popular Models and Unhappy Experiences............. 55

INTRODUCTION

The first part of this book combines four essays on
Brazilian economic development. It explores the effects of
fiscal, monetary and trade policies on growth, inflation and
distribution. It asks questions that Brazilian economists
have been worrying about for a long time:

Was industrialization linked to unfavorable conditions
in the external sector and exchange devaluations? Did the
coffee-support policies contribute to industrialization
during the thirties? What were the effects of a balanced budget
purchase of coffee on trade account and income? Did quotas on
the importation of consumer goods have a positive effect on
capital accumulation during the forties? How do minidevaluations
and wage indexation interact and modify the impact of fiscal and
monetary policies on growth, inflation and distribution?

It is simpler to deal with these questions by using analyt-
ical models, easy to build up from elements that the toll
kit of economists provides. This is particularly true when one
is aware that economic models, like machines, despite their great
variety of shapes and uses, can be handled as combinations of

few elementary mechanisms. Ammendments can then be made by reordering the parts in the light of perceived peculiarities of a given economic context, and by seizing upon the lessons produced by the constant experimentation of policy makers.

Although formal models might be helpful in working out answers, understanding of economic facts cannot be derived from an immediate application of general principles. It requires a scrutiny of the concrete historical setting in which these facts are rooted. Working out from real life situations discourages the mystifying notion of the economy as a territory impervious to politics.

The first chapter develops a model for the exchange rate in Brazil during the second half of the nineteenth century. The exchange rate discussion has a bearing in the sources of industrialization in Brazil. Two explanations stem from a primary export base. Whereas the "adverse shock argument" links industrialization to unfavorable conditions in the external sector and exchange devaluations, the alternative approach views industrialization from the standpoint of the growth of income brought by the rise in exports. Those mechanisms are discussed. Also considered are the effects of monetary policy and the behavior of wages. The evidence shows that purchasing power parity is not enough to explain the exchange rate behavior, which clearly responded to coffee export revenues.

The second chapter discusses the role of fiscal and monetary policies in an LDC with a major commodity export that is facing a depression abroad. The analysis is conducted in the context of a general equilibrium model which comprises a commodity-producing sector and an import-competing sector. Idle capacity and labor unemployment are assumed. Flexibility of the real exchange rate and industrial output responses to demand are the main adjusting mechanisms. The key to understanding the behavior of the Brazilian economy in the 1930s is the government coffee-support policy, which held the income of the export sector at a high level and hence enabled the manufacturing sector to expand. The fact that industrial output expanded in the face of both real depreciation and appreciation points to the importance of expenditure effects relative to price effects during the 1930s.

The third chapter investigates the trade policies of the postwar period. Quantitative restrictions on consumer goods imports led to an increase both in their prices and in the rate of profit on the domestic industrial activity. Investment theory tells us that capital growth depends on profitability. So it happened during the late forties. Lack of a coherent plan led at the same time to a discrimination against the agricultural sector and growing inequality of income.

The next chapter examines how external financing of trade deficits during the seventies permitted Brazil to increase her productive capacity. The model presented brings into the center of the argument the question of the division of output between the classes of society, stressing the political element in economic development. It incorporates indexed wages and their interplay with minidevaluations together with the effects these policies had on growth, inflation and the functional distribution of income, during the past decade. The persistent surplus of imports has led to the debt problem of the eighties.

The second part of the book moves our attention to a broader context. High inflation rates and balance of payments crises are the everyday experience of Latin Americans. Stabilization policies that cut down on growth performance, the inevitable medicine. Periods of growth and low inflation occur at the same time as trade deficits and abundant external credit, and are followed by balance of payments crisis. To cut on imports and promote exports, governments then reduce growth and devalue the exchange rate. But devaluations are inflationary. Thus, policies designed to restore external balance ultimately give little help with growth but always lead to more inflation.

The interpretations of Latin American stabilization experiences are not necessarily exclusive, although different models and

different schools of thought emphasize different aspects of
the same problem. Economists of a more conservative strand
tend to believe that adjustment costs are short lived. Others
would emphasize that economies take time to adjust to changes
in relative prices and that in the meantime wage earners bear
most of the burden of adjustment. During a stabilization program
à la IMF, wage earners have to live with more unemployment and
lower real wages until capital moves to the traded goods sector,
which becomes more profitable thanks to the exchange rate devaluations. Until then, falling standards of living and political
unrest become an important ingredient of such experiments.

The last chapter surveys popular models of economic
stabilization in developing countries, and compares the
experience of different Latin American countries during
periods of stabilization over the past three decades.

PART I

ESSAYS ON ECONOMIC HISTORY IN BRAZIL

CHAPTER I

EXCHANGE RATES IN NINETEENTH-CENTURY BRAZIL

I. INTRODUCTION

This paper studies the behavior of the Brazilian exchange rate from 1862 to 1906. Figure 1 depicts the nominal exchange rate and the real price of imports during the years covered between the National Exposition of 1861, which signaled the rise of an industrial spirit in Brazil, and the opening of the Caixa de Conversão, which ended the period of flexible exchange rates, in 1906. The empirical evidence, in section II, shows that purchasing power parity is not enough to explain the exchange rate behavior, which clearly responded to coffee export revenues.

Section I develops a model for the exchange rate. It implies that the determination of the exchange rate, flexible during the period in question, depended on the overall balance of payments position and therefore, on export revenues and expenditures on imports. In the last fifty years of the nineteenth century, export revenues derived mainly from coffee.[1] The price of coffee was established in the international market, but because of the Brazilian monopoly, it was mainly a function of the quantity Brazil offered for sale. Expenditures on imports were determined by the relative price of imports and by the level of domestic activity which, in turn, rested on monetary policy and the wage level. These were also the determinants of the rate of profit and therefore, of equipment imports. Thus, the model predicts that the coffee price, export revenues, expenditures on imports and the exchange rate were basically determined by the behavior of wages, by

---

1. The exchange rate behavior and its relationships with coffee, during the period in question, have been considered by Furtado [*1959*], Fishlow [*1972*], Stein [*1979*] and Versiani [*1980*].

Figure 1

THE NOMINAL EXCHANGE RATE AND THE REAL PRICE OF IMPORTS
BRAZIL: 1860-1913

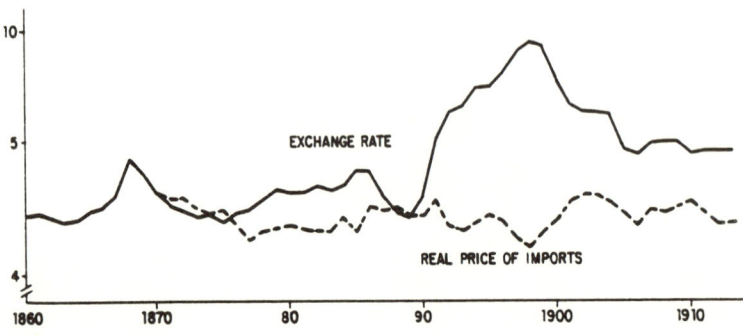

SOURCE: See Appendix.

monetary policy and by the quantities of coffee sold abroad, (and increasingly, toward the end of the century, by the quantities of exported rubber).[2] This theoretical explanation of the behavior of the exchange rate is not rejected by our tests, as we shall demonstrate in section II.

II. THE MODEL

The economy to be analyzed has two sectors—a primary export sector and an industrial sector. There are two types of imported goods: capital goods, K, which serve as inputs for domestic manufacturers, and consumer goods, M, which compete against domestic similars, Q, in the home market. The supplies of imported capital and consumer goods are assumed to be perfectly elastic at their international prices, P_K^* and P_m^*. The prices of these goods in *cruzeiros* are: $P_K \equiv eP_K^*$ and $P_m \equiv eP_m^*$, where e stands for the exchange rate. The *cruzeiro* price of domestic similars is $P = P_m$,[3] and assuming that $P_K^* \equiv P_m^* \equiv 1$, it follows that $P_K = P_m = P = e$. The *cruzeiro* price of exports is P_x. Measured in terms of industrial consumer goods, the real price of exports is $P_x \equiv P_x/P$. Real income is: $y \equiv p_x X + Q$, where $p_x X$ is the income generated in the export sector, and Q is the industrial output.

We first look at the demand for imported goods. Consumer goods imports are equal to the demand for consumer goods, D, which depends on real income, less domestic supply, Q:

$$M = D(y) - Q(w, K) \qquad (1)$$

The supply of domestic manufactures depends on the real wage, w, and on the stock of capital, since the product is obtained by combining labor and

---
2. Between 1895 and 1910, coffee and rubber exports were responsible for 55.5 per cent and 24 per cent of total export revenues, respectively.
3. This equation is equivalent to the hypothesis that domestically produced and imported consumer goods are perfect substitutes. A less-than-perfect substitution hypothesis might be added to the model, using equations representing demand as a function of relative prices and an equation representing equilibrium in the market for domestic goods in place of equation (2). The possibility of less-than-perfect substitution is left aside because the focus is on exchange rate determination and not on the import substitution problem.

imported capital. The real wage, paid by the producer[4] is defined as:

$$w \equiv W/P$$

Investment, or capital goods imports, depends on the difference between the rate of profit in the industrial sector, π, and the rate of interest, r:[5]

$$\frac{dK}{dt} = \sigma(\pi - r) \qquad (2)$$

The profits of the manufacturing sector are calculated as the value of industrial product less the wage bill. The rate of profit is obtained by dividing the profits by the value of the stock of capital:

$$\pi = (Q(w,K) - wL(w,K))/K \qquad (3)$$

where $L \equiv$ industrial employment.

The rate of interest behaves in accordance with the money market. The money market is in equilibrium when the real supply of money, H/P, is equal to the demand. Assuming that the demand for real cash depends on the interest rate, r, and on real wealth, defined as: $R \equiv (H/P) + K$, we can write that $H/P = \lambda(r)R$, or:

$$r = \lambda^{-1}(h) \qquad (4)$$

where: $h \equiv H/(H + PK)$.

Substituting (3) and (4) into (2) and observing that, if the rate of profit is the same as the rate of interest, the stock of capital remains constant (that is, $dK/dt = 0$), we obtain:

$$Q(w, K) - wL(w, K) - \lambda^{-1}(h)K = 0 \qquad (5)$$

Equation (2) describes capital accumulation as a rising function of the

---

4. It is necessary to distinguish between the real wage paid by the employer and that received by the worker. For the employer, the real wage is the nominal wage, W, deflated by the price of his product, P; but for the worker, the wage is deflated by the price of the goods he consumes. What can be said concerning the latter during the period in question?
  Referring to the second half of the nineteenth century, Stein [1979] observes that the industrial labor force was recruited against the background of a slave society. Even after abolition, the situation of former slaves and European immigrant workers changed little. Despite the fact that manufacturers sometimes mentioned labor shortages, there is no indication that such shortages held back industrial growth. Workers were recruited from orphanages, charity institutions, and from among the unemployed in the coastal towns. Still according to Stein, manufacturers often stated that labor was cheap, a contention which is apparently backed by the large number of women and children employed.
  This description is in accord with the hypothesis that the real wage received by the worker was determined by the subsistence level. Assuming that the model implicitly contains a subsistence sector, and also assuming that prices of subsistence goods are given exogenously, it follows that the nominal wage, proportional to the price of the subsistence goods, are also determined exogenously. The effects of an increase in the price of subsistence goods, and therefore in the nominal and real wages are discussed below.
5. Equation (2) describes net investment. If $\pi < r$, net investment is negative; that is, the equipment imported is not sufficient to offset the wear on the existing stock of capital.

difference between the rate of profit and the rate of interest. When these two rates are equal (equation (5)) the stock of capital is constant. In Figure 2, this relationship is described by the curve KK, whose positive slope is explained as follows. Assume the exchange rate and the stock of capital are such that

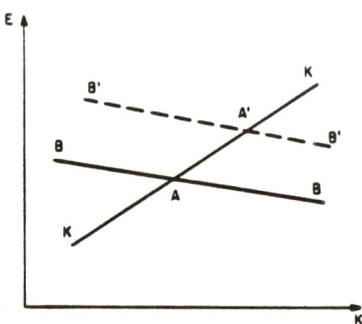

Figure 2

A DECREASE IN EXPORT REVENUES

the rate of profit and the interest rate are equal. An exchange devaluation raises the price of industrial goods, bringing about reductions in both the real wage and real cash balances. The drop in the real wage increases the rate of profit, while that in real balances pushes up the rate of interest. For the devaluation to occasion an increase in the stock of capital, it must have a stronger impact on the rate of industrial profits than on the rate of interest. The likelihood of this occuring is greater, the greater the share of labor costs in industrial product and the less elastic the equilibrium rate of interest with respect to the ratio of real balances to real wealth.

Internal and External Equilibrium

Internal and external equilibrium are observed if income equals expenditures, i.e., if the trade balance, B, is zero:

$$B = x - dK/dt - M = 0 \qquad (6)$$

where: $x \equiv p_x X$

External equilibrium, guaranteed by the flexibility of the exchange rate, is depicted by the curve BB in Figure 2. The negative slope of BB is explained as follows. Assume that the exchange rate and the stock of capital are initially such that the trade balance is in equilibrium. An increase in the stock of capital affects both consumer and capital goods imports. On the one hand, a large stock of capital allows manufacturers to increase their production of consumer goods. This reduces consumer goods imports, since expenditures rise less than proportionally to income. On the other hand, a larger stock of capital means a lower rate of profit, and consequently less imports for investment purposes. It follows that a stock of capital larger than that held at the outset is linked to a balance-of-trade surplus. For equilibrium to be re-established, the exchange rate must appreciate.

In Figure 2, both internal and external equilibrium obtain at point A (where KK and BB intersect). The equilibrium relationships are subject to modification by changes in export revenues, in international prices of import goods, in the wage rate, and by monetary expansions. We can thus write the equilibrium exchange rate as:

$$e = e(x, P^*, W, H) \qquad (7)$$

In what follows we examine the effect on the exchange rate of changes in our exogenous variables.

Adverse Shocks

In the literature, an adverse shock is defined as a drop in export revenues which leads to a trade deficit. With the existing stock of capital, lower export revenues mean that external equilibrium can only be achieved at a higher exchange rate (see Figure 2). The exchange rate depreciates, raising the price of consumer goods. This, in turn, encourages the domestic production of such goods and diminishes the trade deficit. Note that the exchange depreciation not only lowers real wages, but also forces up the rate of interest. Since we are assuming that the depreciation exerts a stronger effect on wages than on the financial market, the rate of profit rises in relation to the rate of interest, thus stimulating investment. In final equilibrium, the stock of capital is larger than at the outset.

A Monetary Expansion

A monetary expansion lowers the rate of interest and encourages investment. The increase in capital goods imports generates a trade deficit, and the exchange rate depreciates. The stock of capital grows in response to the exchange depreciation and the lower interest rate.

Wage Increases

A wage increase lowers the rate of profit and discourages investment. Since the stock of capital decreases in response to the fall in the rate of profit, domestic manufacturing slows down. Consumer goods imports mount, so the balance of payments can be held in equilibrium only if there is an exchange depreciation.[6]

---

6. The impact of a monetary expansion coupled with a proportional wage increase, induce an exchange rate depreciation in the same proportion as the money supply and the nominal wage increase, leaving the stock of capital unchanged.

An Increase in International Prices

The general level of prices abroad is denoted P^*. A rise in international prices, such that $\hat{P}_M^* = \hat{P}_K^* = \hat{P}^*$, causes a proportional drop in the exchange rate, but does not alter the stock of capital. (In terms of Figure 2, this exercise is equivalent to a downward shift, proportional to the increase in the general price level abroad, of the curves KK and BB.)

The exercises presented show that the exchange rate and the stock of capital are determined simultaneously as functions of variations in monetary holdings, wages, export revenues and international prices. When the relative price of consumer goods and capital goods remains constant, monetary expansion, coupled with the behavior of wages and exports, are sufficient to explain the behavior of the exchange rate and the stock of capital. In the next section, we survey the empirical evidence for the period 1862–1906, during which Brazil had a flexible exchange rate.

III. EMPIRICAL EVIDENCE

In this section, we survey the empirical evidence concerning the behavior of the exchange rate in the latter half of the nineteenth century. Using the model developed above, the exchange rate can be determined as a function of the money supply (H), the wage rate (W), export revenues (x) and international prices (P^*).[7] We re-write equation (7) as:

$$Lne = \alpha_0 + \alpha_1 LnW + \alpha_2 LnH + \alpha_3 Lnx + \alpha_4 LnP^*$$

The theory predicts that $\alpha_1 > 0, \alpha_2 > 0, \alpha_1 + \alpha_2 = 1, \alpha_3 < 0, \alpha_4 = -1$, as illustrated by the preceding exercises.

The equation for the exchange rate was estimated for Brazil for the periods 1862–1906 and 1870–1906, which excludes the years of the Paraguayan War. We shall now describe the statistical information[8] and discuss our findings.

---

7. An implicit hypothesis is that variations in the relative price between imported capital and consumer goods were of little importance in comparison to variations in wages, in the money supply and in export revenues.
8. For a detailed description of the series used, see the Appendix.

The exchange rate, together with export revenues in pounds sterling, was taken from FIBGE. The money supply corresponds to the annual average of M_1 (money in circulation plus cash deposits) given in Villela and Suzigan [*1973*]. Owing to the lack of information on wages, food prices were used as a proxy. To avoid errors due to the possibility of sharp fluctuations in food prices, we used a three-year moving average of the cost-of-living index calculated by Lobo et al. [*1971*]. To obtain real export revenues, export earnings should be deflated by a price index for Brazilian imports. Since no such index exists,[9] we adopted the general price index for England given in Deane and Cole [*1967*]. As England was Brazil's major trade partner in the period, this index is used to represent world prices.

It should be noted that the ordinary least-squares method is not suited to estimating the equations for the exchange rate due to the problem of simultaneity. In the first place, export revenues in pounds sterling depend on the international coffee price, which is determined simultaneously with the exchange rate. Second, the cost-of-living index, used as a proxy for the nominal wage, comprises nine elements, of which three are imported goods. Third, it could be argued that the money supply was determined by a rule that took exchange fluctuations into account.

These problems were overcome by estimating the equations via the instrumental variable method. Two alternative hypotheses were formulated.

TABLE 1

$Lne = \alpha_0 + \alpha_1 LnW + \alpha_2 LnH + \alpha_3 Lnx + \alpha_4 LnP^*$.
Instrumental variables: $LnH, LnH_{-1}, LnP^*, LnQC, LnQC_{-1}, LnQB, LnQB_{-1}, T$

	α_0	α_1	α_2	α_3	α_4	R^2	DW	SER	Rho
1. 1870–1906	6.16	0.57	0.55	−0.62	−0.83	0.98	1.95	0.07	0.03
	(6.75)	(8.16)	(8.54)	(−8.65)	(−5.03)				
2. 1862–1906	5.34	0.66	0.37	−0.42	−0.77	0.96	2.24	0.08	0.85
	(2.39)	(3.53)	(3.37)	(−3.38)	(−1.91)				

TABLE 2

$Lne = \alpha_0 + \alpha_1 LnW + \alpha_2 LnH + \alpha_3 Lnx + \alpha_4 LnP^*$.
Instrumental variables: $LnH_{-1}, LnP^*, LnQC, LnQC_{-1}, LnQB, LnQB_{-1}, T$

	α_0	α_1	α_2	α_3	α_4	R^2	DW	SER	Rho
1. 1870–1906	6.11	0.51	0.65	−0.71	−0.77	0.97	1.99	0.07	−0.05
	(6.67)	(6.82)	(8.33)	(−8.69)	(−4.58)				
2. 1862–1906	4.91	0.60	0.49	0.44	−0.73	0.96	2.32	0.08	0.87
	(2.12)	(2.86)	(2.73)	(−3.29)	(−1.75)				

NOTE: The equations were estimated using the instrumental variables method and corrected by Fair's method. The t-statistics are in parentheses.

---

9. There is an index for textile imports as of 1870 calculated by Versiani [*1980*].

In Table 1, the equations were estimated on the assumptions that the money supply is exogenous. The instruments used were the current and lagged money supply, the current and lagged quantities of coffee and rubber exported, and time. In Table 2, the equations were estimated on the assumption that money is endogenous. The instruments were the same, except for the current money supply.

The equations are reproduced in Table 1 and behave extremely well, especially for the period 1870–1906.[10] All the coefficients have the expected signs and are accurately estimated. Above all, the following hypotheses cannot be rejected: $\alpha_1 + \alpha_2 = 1$ and $\alpha_4 = -1$. The evidence shows that purchasing power parity is not enough to explain the exchange rate behavior which clearly responded to coffee export revenues.

---

10. It may be that the equations for the period 1862–1906 performed less well due to the inclusion of the years 1864–1870, during which the Paraguayan War took place. However, the coefficient of a dummy variable introduced into the exchange rate equations for these years was not significant.

APPENDIX

Statistical Information

In the following, the variables used in the regressions and in Figure 1 are described and their sources are given:

1. Rate of exchange, e:

The log of the index of the average annual rate of exchange, given in FIBGE [*1939/40: 1353–4*], was used.

2. Real export revenues, x:

The log of the index of total export revenues in pounds sterling, x, was deflated by the general price index for England, P^*. The source of the forementioned log is FIBGE [*1939/40: 1358–9*].

3. Money supply, H:

The average annual stock was calculated on the basis of the trimestral data presented by Peláez and Suzigan [*1976: 465–77*].

4. Wages, W:

The log of the three-year moving average of the Rio de Janeiro cost-of-living index (1919 weight) was used. This index is from Lobo *et al.* [*1971: 260–2*].

5. Quantity of coffee exported, QC:

The index for the quantity of coffee exported was calculated from data published in FIBGE [*1939/40: 1375*].

6. Quantity of rubber exported, QB:

The index for the quantity of rubber exported was calculated from data published in FIBGE [*1939/40: 1376*].

7. General price index for England, P^*:

This price index is the implicit deflator of the product of the United Kingdom in Deane and Cole [*1967: 329–30*]. It was used to deflate equipment imports and to obtain the real value of Brazilian exports.

8. Real price of imports:

The index for real price of imports was calculated as $(1+\tau)P_m/P$, where $(1+\tau)$ = the tariff protection index calculated by Versiani [*1980: 36*]; P_m = the index for the *mil-réis* price of textile imports calculated by Versiani [*1980: 36*]; P = Lobo [*1980*] index, 1919 weight. The log of the index for the real price of imports, together with the log of the index of the nominal exchange rate, is depicted in Figure 1.

REFERENCES

Deane. P. and W. Cole. 1967. *British Economic Growth, 1688–1959.* Cambridge University Press.
FIBGE. *Annuário Estatistico do Brasil,* Ano V—1939/40. Rio de Janeiro: Fundação Instituto Brasileiro de Geografia e Estatistica.
Fishlow. A.. 1972. 'Origens e Consequências da Substituição de Importações no Brasil'. *Estudos Econômicos,* 2(6).
Furtado. C.. 1959. *Formação Econômica do Brasil,* Rio de Janeiro: Fundação de Cultura.
Lobo. E. *et al..* 1971. 'Evolução dos Preços e Padrão de Vida no Rio de Janeiro—Resultados Preliminares'. *Revista Brasileira de Economia*, 25 (4).
Pelaéz. C. and W. Suzigan. 1976. *História Monetária do Brasil,* Rio de Janeiro: IPEA. Nonograph: 23.
Stein. S.. 1979. *Origens e Evolução da Indústria Textil no Brasil, 1850–1950.* Rio de Janeiro: Editora Campos.
Versiani. F.. 1980. 'Industrialização e Economia de Exportação: A Experiência Brasileira antes de 1914'. *Revista Brasileira de Economia,* 34 (1).

CHAPTER II

THE GREAT DEPRESSION AND THE BRAZILIAN COFFEE-SUPPORT POLICY

This paper discusses the role of fiscal and monetary policies in an LDC with a major commodity export facing a depression abroad. The analysis is conducted in the context of a general equilibrium model which comprises a commodity-producing sector and an import-competing sector that produces both consumption and investment goods. Idle capacity and labor unemployment are assumed. Flexibility of the real exchange rate and industrial output response to demand are the main adjusting mechanisms.

Having presented the model in the first section, we use it as the basis of our discussion of industrialization in Brazil in the years of the Great Depression. The key to understanding the behavior of the Brazilian economy in the 1930s is the government coffee-support policy, which held the income of the export sector at a high level and hence enabled the manufacturing sector to expand.[1] We show that stockpiling expanded income, and that, when stockpiling was financed by export duties, the trade balance improved, but when it was financed by credit, a trade deficit arose. The fact that the currency was devalued during periods in which the coffee sector was supported through domestic credit expansion but appreciated when coffee purchases were financed via duties strengthens the hypothesis that devaluations were a response to the external disequilibrium created by the coffee policy. The fact that industrial output expanded in the face of both real depreciation and appreciation points to the importance of expenditures effects, relative to depreciation and price effects, induced by fiscal and monetary policies during the 1930s.

I. The Model

The economy has two sectors: a coffee-producing sector oriented to the export market and a manufacturing sector that produces goods for domestic consumption and investment. Imported goods compete with domestic manufactures on the internal market.

There are markets for three types of goods: coffee (C), domestic manufactures (Q), and imported manufactures (M). The prices of these goods in home currency are, respectively, P_c, P, and P_m. The nominal wage is denoted W. The world supply of imported manufactures is perfectly elastic at the international price P_m^*, so that $P_m = eP_m^*$, where e stands for the exchange rate.

When imported manufactures are used as the numeraire, the *real*

---

[1] This hypothesis is advanced by Furtado (1963). Furtado is criticized by Peláez (1972), who contends that a large share of the income generated by the multiplier effects of the coffee-support expenditures was canceled by the offsetting negative multiplier effects of the taxes levied to finance coffee purchases. Fishlow (1972) argues that the coffee-support program generated demand in a somewhat more complex manner than Furtado believes. Basing his argument on a partial equilibrium model, Fishlow maintains that the greater part of the export duties were passed on to the foreign consumer. The transfers of the duties was guaranteed by the inelasticity of demand and the high elasticity of supply. Our more complete model incorporates the mechanism described by Fishlow, while at the same time analyzing the coffee policy from the standpoint of its impact on real income in accord with the approach advised by Peláez and Suzigan (1976). A monetary explanation for the industrial upsurges during the 1930s is found in Peláez (1972) and Neuhaus (1973). The monetary factors explaining the behavior of economic policy in the Brazilian experience during the Depression are also incorporated in our model.

prices are: $p_c = P_c/P_m$, $p = P/P_m$, and $w = W/P_m$. We assume unemployment and a given nominal wage rate.

A. The Coffee Market

In the coffee sector, the fixed factor (suitable land planted in coffee and served by adequate transport) can be combined with varying quantities of labor to obtain the crop. The grower maximizes profits by equalizing the value of the marginal product and a given nominal wage. When the price of coffee rises, so do employment and output. The coffee supply is, therefore, a rising function of the price of coffee in wage units:

$$C^s = C^s(p_c/w). \qquad (1)$$

Coffee is exported. Foreign demand is a function of the real income of the coffee-importing countries, y^*, and of the dollar price of coffee deflated by the world price of imported manufactures:

$$C^D = C^D(T\tilde{p}_c, y^*), \qquad (2)$$

where $\tilde{p}_c = (P_c/eP_m^*)$ and $T = 1 + t$, with t being the duty rate on coffee exports and P_c and P_m^* the home price of coffee and foreign currency price of manufactures.

Part of the coffee is bought by the government rather than sold abroad. These purchases are financed through foreign loans, domestic credit, and export duties on coffee. The real coffee purchases on the part of the government are designated G.

Equilibrium on the coffee market requires that[2]

$$C^s(p_c/w) = C^D(\tilde{p}_c T, y^*) + G. \qquad (3)$$

Equation (3) determines the real producers' price of coffee, p_c, as a function of the exogenous variables:[3] $p_c = p_c(y^*, G, T, w)$; $\partial p_c/\partial y^* > 0$; $\partial p_c/\partial G > 0$; $\partial p_c/\partial T < 0$; and $\partial p_c/\partial w > 0$.

We also define real export earnings, X, and real disposable income of the coffee sector, y_c, measured in terms of imported manufactures, respectively, as:[4]

---

[2] It is assumed that domestic coffee consumption is negligible.
[3] From (3):

$$p_c' = \frac{1}{\epsilon_c + \eta_c}(\epsilon_c w' + \eta_{y^*} \cdot y^{*'} + \sigma - \eta_c T'), \qquad (4)$$

where a prime beside the variable indicates its logarithmic derivative, i.e., $x' = dx/x$; $\sigma = dG/C^d$; ϵ_c = price elasticity of the coffee supply; η_c = absolute value of the price elasticity of the demand for coffee; and η_{y^*} = income elasticity of the demand for coffee. Equation (4) is an approximation. It is exactly correct only if initially $G = 0$ or $C^s = C^d$.

[4] The effect of changes in the exogenous variables on real export earnings can be

$$X = Tp_c C^D(Tp_c, y^*) = X(y^*, G, T, w), \qquad (7)$$

$$y_c = p_c C^s(p_c/w) = y_c(y^*, G, T, w). \qquad (8)$$

Real export earnings and real disposable income of the coffee sector are increasing functions of foreign income, government purchases, and real wages. A rise in export taxes raises export earnings but reduces disposable income.

An increase in the real income of the coffee-importing countries, y^*, enhances external coffee demand and raises the real price of coffee, real export earnings, and real disposable income of the coffee sector.

An increase in government coffee purchases boosts the price, and, since the demand for coffee is inelastic, export earnings and real income of the coffee sector rise.

An increase in export duties, T, raises the dollar price and reduces international demand for coffee, bringing on a decrease of the real price received by the grower. Since the demand for coffee is inelastic relative to its price, export earnings rise. But disposable income of the coffee sector falls, because both the quantity produced and the price received by the grower diminish.

An increase in the real wage rate lessens coffee supply and pushes the real price of coffee up. Both export earnings and real income rise inasmuch as demand is inelastic.

B. *The Market for Domestic Manufactures*

The price of domestic manufactures is cost determined. The real price of domestic manufactures, in terms of imported manufactures, is

$$p = \beta w, \qquad (9)$$

where β stands for the output/labor ratio.

Manufacturing output is determined by demand, which depends on real domestic income, y, on its price in relation to that of imported similars, p, and on real balances, h. Real domestic manufacturing output, y_q, thus is:

$$y_q = pQ(p, y, h). \qquad (10)$$

---

studied using the following equation:

$$X' = \left(\frac{1-\eta_c}{\epsilon_c + \eta_c}\right)(\epsilon_c w' + \sigma + \epsilon_c T') + \left(\frac{1+\epsilon_c}{\epsilon_c + \eta_c}\right)\eta_y y^{*'}. \qquad (5)$$

The effect of changes in the exogenous variables on the income of the coffee sector is given by:

$$y_c' = \left(\frac{1+\epsilon_c}{\epsilon_c + \eta_c}\right)(\eta_y y^{*'} + \sigma - \eta_c T') + \left(\frac{\epsilon_c}{\epsilon_c + \eta_c}\right)(1 - \eta_c)w'. \qquad (6)$$

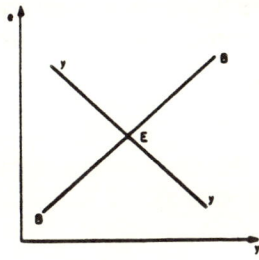

FIG. 1

Real income is defined as:

$$y = y_c + y_q \tag{11}$$

Equations (9), (10), and (11) allow us to determine internal equilibrium and to express real income as a function of the income of the coffee sector, real balances, and the real wage.[5] Given the money stock, the fiscal policy, and the money wage, we can depict internal equilibrium by an inverse relationship between real income and the exchange rate, as illustrated in figure 1 by schedule yy.[6] Assume an initial combination of the real income and the exchange rate for which there is internal equilibrium. An increase in the exchange rate reduces the real wage, real balances, and income of the coffee sector. Both the reduction in real balances and the reduction in the income of the coffee sector contribute to reducing the demand for domestic goods. However, the reduction in real wages, and thus in the price of domestic goods in relation to imports, increases demand for domestic manufactures in substitution for the imported goods. As long as the two first effects dominate, a depreciation of the exchange rate reduces demand for domestic manufactures. Consequently, industrial output

---

[5] Assuming that, initially, $G = t = 0$ and $X = M$, where M stands for imports, we have: $y_c = X = M$ and, from eq. (11),

$$dy/M = y_c' + (y_q/M)y_q' \tag{12}$$

From eq. (10),

$$y_q' = (1 - \eta_q)p' + q(dy/y_q) + \lambda_q h', \tag{13}$$

where: η_q = absolute value of the price elasticity of the demand for domestic manufactures; q = marginal propensity to consume domestic manufactures; and λ_q = elasticity of demand for domestic manufactures in relation to real balance. Substituting (13) into (12) and observing, from the budget constraint, that $(y_q/M)(1 - \eta_q) = \eta_m$, where η_m is the price elasticity of the demand for imported manufactures, we obtain:

$$dy/M = [1/(1 - q)](y_c' - \eta_m p' + \Theta\lambda_q h'), \tag{14}$$

where $\Theta = y_q/M$.

[6] Note that $h' = p' = w = -e'$, for given nominal money stock and nominal rate. For given policy, we also have: $y_c' = \phi_c w'$, where $\phi_c = (1 - \eta_c)[\epsilon_c/(\epsilon_c + \eta_c)]$. We can thus rewrite (14) as $e'/(dy/M) = -(s + m)/(\phi_c + \Theta\lambda_q - \eta_m)$, where s = the marginal propensity to save. The schedule yy is downward sloping as long as $(\phi_c + \Theta\lambda_q) > \eta_m$.

falls, and real income is reduced. It is implied that a depreciation is contractionary when the nominal money supply is held constant.

C. The Balance of Payments

Imports of manufactures, M, are a function of their price relative to that of domestic similar products, of real income, and of real cash balances:

$$M = M(p, y, h). \qquad (15)$$

The balance of payments measured in terms of imported manufactures is

$$B = X - M + F, \qquad (16)$$

where F stands for independent movements of foreign capital expressed in terms of imported goods.

External equilibrium, $B = 0$, can be represented by a positive relationship between the exchange rate and real income, as illustrated by schedule BB in figure 1.[7] If real income increases, the demand for imports rises, generating a trade deficit. To restore equilibrium, the exchange rate has to depreciate. For the depreciation to improve the balance of payments, the reduction in coffee-export revenues has to be smaller than the reduction in import spending, obtained through the substitution effect, and the reduction in cash balances, induced by the depreciation.

As illustrated in figure 1, internal and external equilibrium prevails at E, where yy and BB cross. We shall now illustrate the model by presenting some historically relevant comparative static exercises.

D. Coffee Purchases Financed by Export Duties

Assuming that $G = t = 0$, at the outset, the result of the government's increasing expenditures while maintaining a balanced budget ($dG = dtC^D$) is as follows.

Since the demand for coffee is inelastic, the initial impact of government outlays financed by export duties is to raise coffee prices and export earnings,[8] creating a trade surplus and shifting BB to the right,[9] as in figure 2. On the other hand, as the income of the coffee

---

[7] To obtain the slope of BB, we assume $B = 0$, $X = M$, and $F = 0$, at the outset. We thus differentiate (16) totally to obtain $e'/(dy/M) = m/(\eta_m + \lambda_m - \phi_e)$: m = the marginal propensity to spend in imported manufactures; and λ_m = the elasticity of demand for imports in relation to real balances.

[8] Observe that $dX = dy_c = \{(1 + \epsilon_c)[(1 - \eta_c)/(\epsilon_c + \eta_c)]\}P_c dG$.

[9] The schedule BB shifts to the right in the following proportion: $dy = (1/m)dX$.

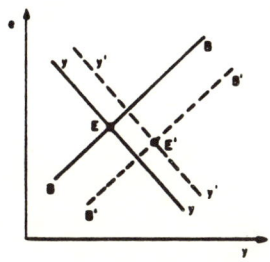

Fig. 2

sector rises, the demand for manufactures is promoted, and industrial production expands (yy shifts to the right).[10] At the higher income level, there still is a trade surplus.[11] The higher the marginal propensity to save, the larger is the balance-of-payments surplus, because less expenditures on foreign manufactures will be induced by the higher domestic income. The exchange rate appreciates to correct for the external surplus.

We thus conclude that coffee purchases financed by export duties are expansionary and induced an appreciation of the exchange rate.

E. *Coffee Purchases Financed by Foreign Loans*

Next, we consider coffee purchases financed by foreign loans. As in the preceding case, increases occur in the price of coffee, in export earnings, and in income of the coffee sector. Likewise, industrial output expands, and domestic income grows. With the increase in imports, a trade deficit lower than the government deficit arises. Since the government deficit is offset by foreign loans, the balance of payments improves. Coffee purchases financed by foreign loans are, thus, expansionary and induce an appreciation of the exchange rate, ceteris paribus.[12]

F. *Coffee Purchases Financed by Printing Money*

Consider, now, coffee purchases financed by printing money ($p_c dG = dh$). As already seen, the increase in government expenditures on

---

[10] The schedule yy shifts to the right in the following proportion: $dy = [1/(s + m)]dy_c$.

[11] At the going exchange rate, the trade surplus can be measured by $dB = [s/(s + m)]dy_c$.

[12] Observe that, when coffee purchases are financed by foreign loans, $dX = [(1 - \eta_c)/(\epsilon_c + \eta_c)]dG$ and $dy_c = [(1 + \epsilon_c)/(\epsilon_c + \eta_c)]dG$. In terms of our figures, yy shifts to the right in the following proportion, $dy = [1/(s + m)]dy_c$; and BB shifts to the right in the following proportion, $dy = \{(1/m)[(1 + \epsilon_c)/(\epsilon_c + \eta_c)]\}dF = (1/m)dy_c$.

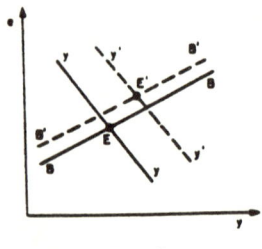

Fig. 3

coffee will raise the price of the product, export earnings, and the income of the coffee sector. Observe that the increase in the income of the coffee sector, for an increase in government expenditures on coffee, is larger than the increase in export revenues since it also grows by the government deficit.

The increase in money balances induces more spending on imports. If this effect exceeds the increase in export revenues, even at the initial income level, a trade deficit appears, shifting BB to the left,[13] as shown in figure 3. On the other hand, at the going exchange rate, the increases in real money balances and in the income of the coffee sector contribute to creating excess demand for domestic goods. Accordingly, the equilibrium output level of the manufacturing sector is enhanced, and real income grows.[14]

At the going exchange rate, a balance-of-payments deficit appears. The external disequilibrium is corrected as the exchange rate depreciates: Domestic goods substitute for imports, and the reduction in real balances reduces demand for both domestic and imported goods.

We thus conclude that financing coffee purchases through credit or duties has far different effects for the balance of payments. The government can also finance its coffee purchases through a combination of duties, credit, and foreign loans. The final effect will certainly be an expansion of income, but the effect on the exchange rate then depends on the shares of credit, export duties, and foreign loans in the total government expenditures on coffee, and on the savings propensity.

II. The 1930s: An Application

Figure 4 exhibits the Brazilian industrial output expansion during the 1930s in the face of alternating real depreciation and appreciation. The model developed in the previous section asserts that the coffee-

---

[13] The shift in BB can be measured by $dy = \{(1/m)[(1 - \eta_c)(\epsilon_c + \eta_m) - \lambda_m(M/h)]\}dh$.
[14] The shift in yy is measured by $dy = \{[1/(s + m)][(1 + \epsilon_c)(\epsilon_c + \eta_c) + (y_q/h)\lambda_q]\}dh$.

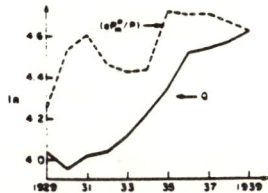

Fig. 4.—Real industrial output and the real exchange rate, Brazil, 1929-39. Source: table 2.

TABLE 1

RATES OF DEPRECIATION IN BRAZIL: 1928-39

Period	$(e - e_{-1})/e_{-1}$
1928-31	.68
1931-33	-.11
1933-35	.37
1935-37	-.07
1937-39	.19

SOURCE.—Table 3.

support policy pursued during the 1930s in Brazil accounts for the industrial output expansion observed in the period. It also follows from the model that the observed appreciation rates, shown in table 1, can be attributed to the fact that, in the periods 1931-33 and 1935-37, stockpiling was mainly financed by export duties, and that the observed depreciations, in the years 1933-34 and 1937-39, can be attributed to the fact that, during those periods, coffee purchases were mainly financed by domestic credit. We further explore these facts in this section.

In the course of the 1920s, the coffee-support program proved quite effective. By purchasing unsalable stocks, the government held the international coffee price at high levels. Because of this artificial stimulus, coffee production nearly doubled from 1925 to 1929 at the same time that export remained approximately constant. In 1927-29, it was possible to export only two-thirds of the harvest.[15]

When the crisis erupted in 1929, both the federal government and the state of São Paulo abandoned their coffee-support programs because the possibility of external financing had vanished, and the Instituto Paulista do Café was in financial straits.[16] Between 1928 and 1930, the coffee price index in cruzeiros fell from 100 to 63.7.[17]

---
[15] See Furtado 1963, p. 198.
[16] See Silber 1977, p. 189.
[17] See Malan and Bonelli 1977, table I.2.

These facts can be fitted into the model presented in Section I. With the relinquishment of the support policy and the drop in the coffee price, both export earnings and domestic income decrease. This, in turn, lowers industrial output (the industrial production index fell from 58 in 1928 to 52 in 1930 [base = 1939])[18] as well as causing expenditures on manufactured imports to decrease more than export earnings. Even so, the trade surplus[19] is outweighed, and the government is forced to devalue the exchange rate in order to deal with the balance-of-payments deficit.

In mid-1930, the São Paulo State government managed to arrange a foreign loan for the purpose of guaranteeing coffee prices,[20] though at this point the mechanism must be qualified because the year 1930 was marked by serious political disturbances and a withdrawal of capital that contributed to the deterioration of the balance of payments as well as to the devaluation of the exchange rate. By assuring minimum purchase prices that were profitable for the majority of the coffee growers, the program actually maintained the employment level of the export economy and, indirectly, of the production sectors linked to the domestic market. Thanks to the coffee policy, industrial production began to recover from its 1930 bottom.

In May 1931, the Conselho Nacional do Café was established to support the coffee sector by purchasing and destroying stocks. The purchases were financed through duties levied on coffee exports and funds obtained from the Banco do Brasil and the National Treasury. In 1931 and 1932, the coffee bought by the government accounted for roughly 30 percent of the export revenues. Between May 1931 and February 1933, 65 percent of these expenditures were financed by duties and the remaining 35 percent by credit from the Banco do Brasil and the National Treasury.[21]

As the income of the coffee sector recovered from its lowest levels thanks to the price-support policy, the increasing demand for manufactures led to a rise in industrial output. Since government expenditures were in part financed by duties, higher income levels were compatible with the improvement in the balance of trade and the appreciation of the exchange rate.

Between February 1933 and December 1934, the shares of the financial sources changed considerably, with domestic credit coming to assume a more important role. To better understand this policy, one might glance at figure 3, where the manufacturing sector expands in the presence of exchange depreciation.

---

[18] See Fishlow 1972, table A-1.
[19] Between 1928 and 1930, export earnings fell from US$473.4 million to US$319.4 million, and imports fell from US$383.3 million to US$225.1 million.
[20] See Silber 1977, p. 190.
[21] Ibid., p. 192.

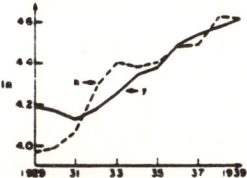

FIG. 5.—Real income and the real money stock, Brazil, 1929–39. Source: table 2.

TABLE 2

REAL OUTPUT, REAL MONEY, AND REAL EXCHANGE RATE INDICES FOR BRAZIL: 1928–39

Years	Index of Real Industrial Output Q (1)	Index of Real Output y (2)	Index of Money Balances Deflated by the GDP Deflator (3)	Index of Import Prices Deflated by Industrial Prices eP_m^*/P (4)
1928	58	65.2	51.5	67.2
1929	56	65.9	52.9	69.9
1930	52	64.5	54.1	91.7
1931	55	62.4	64.8	99.7
1932	56	65.1	72.1	86.2
1933	61	70.9	81.2	83.0
1934	68	77.4	80.2	84.0
1935	77	79.7	81.8	110.6
1936	91	89.3	88.0	110.3
1937	93	93.4	89.2	110.0
1938	96	97.6	101.9	105.5
1939	100	100.0	100.0	100.0

SOURCES.—Col. 1, Fishlow (1972), table A-1. Col. 2, Haddad (1977), pp. 11, 191. Cols. 3 and 4, table 3.

TABLE 3

MONEY STOCK AND PRICE INDICES FOR BRAZIL: 1928–29

Years	Money Stock Annual Average H (1)	Dollar Exchange Rate e (2)	Import Prices eP_m^* (3)	Industrial Prices P (4)	GDP Deflator (5)
1928	52.9	44.3	56.7	84.4	102.7
1929	52.2	44.3	54.6	78.1	98.7
1930	46.8	48.4	59.4	64.8	86.5
1931	49.9	74.5	69.2	69.4	77.0
1932	56.5	73.4	60.1	69.7	78.4
1933	62.2	66.1	59.4	71.6	76.6
1934	65.4	73.4	63.0	75.0	81.5
1935	70.0	90.6	85.7	77.5	85.6
1936	76.5	90.1	91.3	82.8	86.9
1937	84.8	83.9	94.8	86.2	95.1
1938	100.1	91.7	99.0	93.8	98.2
1939	100.0	100.0	100.0	100.0	100.0

SOURCES.—Col. 1, Peláez and Suzigan (1976), table A-3. Col. 2, Malan and Bonelli (1977), table 1.3. Col. 3, ibid., table A.V.12: this is a tariff-inclusive cruzeiro price of imports. Cols. 4 and 5, ibid., table A.V.14.

Between 1935 and 1937, the Departamento Nacional do Café controlled the export supply through a quota system whereby coffee growers were obliged to turn part of their production over to the government for the formation of stocks. This was similar to financing coffee purchases through duties. During this phase there were less financial resources, and the manufacturing sector expanded in the presence of a slight exchange appreciation.

Figures 4 and 5 and tables 1, 2, and 3 summarize the main facts.

References

Fishlow, Albert. "Origins and Consequences of Import Substitution in Brazil." In *International Economics and Development: Essays in Honor of Raúl Prebisch*, edited by Luis Eugenio Di Marco. New York: Academic Press, 1972.

Furtado, Celso. *The Economic Growth of Brazil: A Survey from Colonial to Modern Times*. Translated by Ricardo W. Aguiar and Eric C. Drysdale. Berkeley and Los Angeles: Univ. California Press, 1963.

Haddad, Claudio. "Crescimento do Producto Real Brasileiro, 1900–1947." In *Formação Econômica do Brasil*, edited by Flavio R. Versiani. São Paulo: Edição Saravia, 1977.

Malan, Pedro, and Bonelli, Regis. *Política Econômica Externa e Industrialização Brasil (1939–1952)*. Rio de Janeiro: Inst. Pesquisa Econ. e Soc., 1977.

Neuhaus, Paulo. "The Monetary History of Brazil: 1900–1945." Mimeographed. Univ. Chicago, Dept. Econ., 1973.

Peláez, Carlos M. *História de Industrialização Brasileira: Crítica a Teoría Estruturalista do Brazil*. Rio de Janeiro: Análise e Perspectiva Econ., 1972.

Peláez, Carlos M., and Suzigan, Wilson. *História Monetária do Brasil: Análise da Política, Comportamento e Instituições Monetárias*. Rio de Janeiro: Inst. Pesquisa Econ. e Soc., 1976.

Silber, S. "Análise da Política Econômica e do Comportamento da Economia Brasileira durante o Período 1929–1939." In *Formação Econômica do Brasil*, edited by Flavio R. Versiani. São Paulo: Edição Saravia, 1977.

CHAPTER III

THE POSTWAR YEARS

The relationship between industrialization and agricultural exports in Brazil following World War II has been extensively analyzed by Furtado, Huddle, Fishlow, and Malan et al.[1] The discussion centers on the impact of the antiagricultural bias, enforced through exchange-rate controls, on the level and rate of growth of the economy.

According to Furtado, the expansion of real output in the postwar years was due to the exchange-rate policy and to selective import controls. From his point of view, the fixed exchange rate, coupled with quantitative restrictions—which restructured the import list in favor of intermediate and capital goods—held down the cost of equipment in relation to the prices of domestically produced manufactures. The subsequent rise in industrial profits stimulated investment in the manufacturing sector.

Huddle, on the contrary, considers the exchange-rate policy and the quantitative import restrictions to have lowered both the rate of investment and the growth rate of output. His argument, founded on estimates that indicate extremely slow economic growth, can be partly refuted on the basis of more recently available data that confirm Furtado's initial calculations (see table 1). Huddle also contends that import liberalization, coupled with exchange-rate devaluations, would have been a better policy alternative, given the problems facing the country after the war.

---

[1] Celso Furtado, *Formação econômica do Brasil* (Rio de Janeiro: Fundo de Cultura, 1959); Donald Huddle, "Balanço de pagamentos e controle de câmbio no Brasil: Eficácia, bem-estar e desenvolvimento," *Revista Brasileira de economia* 18 (June 1964): 5–48, and "Furtado on Exchange Control and Economic Development: An Evaluation and Reinterpretation of the Brazilian Case," *Economic Development and Cultural Change* 13 (April 1967): 269–85; Albert Fishlow, "Origins and Consequences of Import Substitution in Brazil," in *Essays in Honor of Paul Prebisch*, ed. E. De Marco (New York: Academic Press, 1972); Pedro Malan et al., *Política econômica externa e industrialização no Brasil (1939/52)* (Rio de Janeiro: Instituto de Pesquisa Econômica Aplicada, 1977).

TABLE 1
AVERAGE REAL GROWTH RATES, BRAZIL, SELECTED PERIODS

Periods	Total	Industrial
1932–39	6.3	10.0
1939–46	4.5	7.4
1946–52	6.2	7.9

SOURCE.—Pedro Malan et al., *Política econômica externa e industrialização no Brasil (1939/52)* (Rio de Janeiro: Instituto de Pesquira Econômica Aplicada, 1977), p. 111.

NOTE.—Using the information above and a correction for terms of trade changes, average per capita real growth during the period 1946–52 is 4%. This figure exceeds the 1% estimated by Huddle.

This essay is an attempt to formalize the discussion outlined above. The model refers to a developing economy whose industrial sector is oriented to the domestic market and is indirectly dependent on coffee exports to increase its capital stock. Domestic manufactures compete with imported goods on the home market.

The comparative static exercises presented in the first section show that whereas import quotas for manufactured consumer goods promote investment in the industrial sector, the effects of nonselective devaluations are ambiguous. In the second section, empirical evidence referring to the postwar period is examined in the light of the model developed in the first, and an evaluation is provided of the Furtado-Huddle controversy on the capital accumulation effects of trade and exchange-rate policies in the 1946–52 period.

I. The Model

The economy has two sectors: a coffee-producing sector (C) oriented to the export market, and an industrial sector that produces manufactures (Q) for domestic consumption. There are two types of imported goods: capital goods (K), which serve as inputs for domestic manufactures, and consumer goods (M), which compete against domestic similars in the home market.

The supplies of imported capital and consumer goods are assumed to be perfectly elastic at their international prices, P^*_k and P^*_m. The prices of these goods in *cruzeiros* are $P_k = eP^*_k$ and $P_m = eP^*_m$, where e stands for the exchange rate set by the government.

The *cruzeiro* prices of coffee and of domestic manufactures are P_C and P, respectively. The nominal wage is institutionally fixed and denoted by W. Measured in terms of the price of domestic consumer goods, the real prices in the economy are

$$p_k = \frac{P_k}{P}, \quad p_c = \frac{P_c}{P}, \quad p_m = \frac{P_m}{P}, \quad \text{and} \quad w = \frac{W}{P}.$$

A. The Coffee Market

In the coffee sector, the fixed factor (suitable land planted in coffee and served by adequate transport) can be combined with varying quantities of labor to obtain the crop. The grower maximizes profits by equalizing the value of the marginal product and the nominal wage.

Foreign demand depends on the income of the coffee-importing countries (y^*) and on the dollar price of coffee in relation to the price of consumer goods in these countries. The coffee market is in equilibrium when there is no excess demand for coffee:[2]

$$C^D(y^*, p_c/p_m) - C^S(p_c/w) = 0. \tag{1}$$

B. The Market for Domestic Manufactures

In the industrial sector, the output is obtained using a combination of labor and imported capital (K). The supply of domestic manufactures depends on the real wage and on the stock of capital. Consumer goods may be either produced in the country or imported. The demand for the domestic item will depend on its price in relation to that of the imported similar and on real domestic income (y).

The market for domestic manufactures is in equilibrium when excess demand is zero:

$$Q^D(p_m, y) - Q^S(w, K) = 0. \tag{2}$$

Real domestic income is the sum of the product of the coffee sector plus that of the industrial sector, both measured in terms of the domestic manufacture:

$$y = p_c C^S + Q^S. \tag{3}$$

C. The Demand for Capital Goods for Investment

Investment (or capital goods imports) depends on the difference be-

---

[2] We assume domestic demand for coffee to be negligible and coffee export taxes to be nonexistent, so that the dollar price of coffee is equal to the producers' price in *cruzeiros* divided by the exchange rate.

tween the rate of profit (π) of the domestic industrial sector and a rate of interest (r) that is assumed to be determined exogenously:

$$\frac{dK}{dt} = \Psi(\pi - r) .$$

The profits of the manufacturing sector are calculated as the value of industrial product less the wage bill. The rate of profit is obtained by dividing the profits by the value of the stock of capital. The stock of capital will remain constant, $(dK/dt) = 0$, if $\pi = r$, or:[3]

$$Q^S(w, K) - wL(w, K) - rp_k K = 0 , \qquad (4)$$

where L = industrial employment.

D. Solution of the Model

The model is easily solved by collecting its equations into a simple diagram. Given the income of the coffee-importing countries, the exchange rate, and the nominal wage, we know the price of coffee and the income of the coffee sector from equation (1). Substituting (3) into (2) we can express equilibrium in the market for domestic manufactures as a function of the capital stock, the real wage rate, and the real price of imported consumer goods.

Equilibrium in the domestic manufactures market is represented in figure 1 by QQ, the slope of which is given by:[4]

$$\left.\frac{\partial w}{\partial K}\right|_{QQ} = \frac{\Theta_k(1 - q)}{\varepsilon_q(1 - q) + \eta_q} \cdot \frac{w}{K} ,$$

---

[3] Equation (4) is a long-run equilibrium condition. We assume that a rise in the equilibrium capital stock will be matched by a rise in society's savings rate sufficient to generate the extra capital. This is obtained from the change in the distribution of income favoring profits, since money wages are constant.

[4] The slope of QQ is calculated as follows: Log differentiation of (2) and (3) yields:

$$\eta_q p'_m + q \cdot (dy/Q^S) + \varepsilon_q w' - \Theta_k K' = 0 , \qquad (2')$$

where η_q is the absolute value of the price elasticity of the demand for domestic manufactures, q is the marginal propensity to consume domestic manufactures, ε_q is the price elasticity of the supply of domestic manufactures, and Θ_k is the elasticity of the supply of domestic manufactures in relation to the capital stock. A prime beside a variable indicates its log derivative. Thus $x' = dx/x$.

$$(dy/Q^S) = \Theta_k K' - \varepsilon_q w' , \qquad (3')$$

for fixed y^*, P_m, and W. Substituting (3') into (2') and noting that as long as P_m and W are fixed $w' = p'_m$, we can write:

$$[\eta_q + \varepsilon_q(1 - q)]w' - \Theta_k(1 - q)K' = 0 . \qquad (5)$$

Equation (4) describes capital accumulation as an increasing function of the difference between the profit rate and the interest rate. The stock of capital is constant when the rate of profits and the rate of interest are the same. Since the rate of profits and the real wage rate are negatively related for a given interest rate, the equilibrium capital stock is higher the lower is the real wage rate. This situation is depicted by a downward-sloped curve in figure 1. Algebraically, the slope of this curve is expressed as:[6]

$$\left.\frac{\partial w}{\partial K}\right|_{KK} = -(\Theta_L \cdot \eta_k) \cdot \frac{w}{K} < 0 ,$$

where Θ_L is the share of wages in industrial output and η_k is the elasticity of industrial employment in relation to the stock of capital.

In figure 1, the price of domestic manufactures and the stock of capital are in equilibrium where KK crosses QQ. This equilibrium will be stable if (1) the price of domestic manufactures rises when there is excess demand for such goods and falls when there is excess supply; (2) net investment (capital goods imports) occurs whenever the profit rate is higher than the interest rate, but the opposite is observed when $\pi < r$.[7]

The operation of the model will now be illustrated with some comparative static exercises that subsequently are used to analyze the postwar experience.

E. Increase in the Income of Coffee-importing Countries

Higher income in the coffee-importing countries will increase the demand for the product and therefore raise the earnings of the coffee sector. In turn, domestic income will grow and increase the demand for domestic manufactures, pushing their price up and shifting QQ to the right.

The rise in the price of the industrial good leads to a fall in the real wage rate; as the profit rate increases, investment enhances the

---

[6] The slope of KK is calculated as follows: Log differentiation of (4) yields:

$$(-\varepsilon_q - \Theta_L + \eta_L \Theta_L)w' - \Theta_L \eta_k K' - \Theta_k p'_k = 0 , \qquad (4')$$

where Θ_L is the share of labor in industrial output; $\Theta_k = (\partial Q^S/\partial K)(K/Q^S) = rp_k(K/Q^S)$; η_L is the absolute value of the demand for labor in relation to the wage rate; and η_k is the elasticity of demand for labor in relation to the stock of capital. Note that $\Theta_L + \Theta_k = 1$ and $\varepsilon_q = \eta_L \Theta_L$; and because P_k and W are fixed, $w' = p'_k$. Thus we can write:

$$w' + \Theta_L \eta_k K' = 0 .$$

[7] We assume that there is an international market for second-hand equipment.

stock of capital. At the new equilibrium, the real wage rate is lower and the stock of capital larger than before.

F. Increase in the Price of Capital Goods

If the price of capital goods rises—whether due to an increase in the dollar price or the institution of customs duties—the profit rate and the capital stock can be held constant only at a lower real wage rate (KK shifts downward).

At the going real wage rate, the profit rate is less than the interest rate, and that induces net disinvestment. As the capital stock decreases, the supply of industrial goods contracts, creating excess demand which is eliminated through a rise in output prices, that is, a fall in the real wage rate. This process goes on until the system reaches a new equilibrium where both the capital stock and the real wage rate are lower than at the outset.

G. Quantitative Restrictions on the Importation of Manufactured Consumer Goods

If the government sets import quotas for manufactured consumer goods, the domestic price of these goods (P_m) will differ from their international price, as expressed in *cruzeiros* (eP^*_m). A new endogenous variable (p_m) enters the model, which must include an equation for equilibrium in the domestic market for imported manufactures:

$$M(p_m, y) - \bar{M} = 0, \qquad (6)$$

where M is the demand for imported manufactures, which depends on their price in relation to that of domestic similars and on domestic income, and $\bar{M}$ is the supply of imported manufactures, which corresponds to the official quota.

To work out the impact on the stock of capital of a reduction in the supply of imported consumer goods, we must take into account that equilibrium in the market for domestic manufactures is now restricted by (6). In figure 2, $\bar{Q}\bar{Q}$ represents the combinations of real wage rates and capital stock for which the market of domestic manufactures clears in the presence of a quota on imported consumer goods.

The slope of $\bar{Q}\bar{Q}$ is given by:[8]

$$\left.\frac{\partial w}{\partial K}\right|_{\bar{Q}\bar{Q}} = \frac{\Theta_k}{\varepsilon_q} > 0.$$

---

[8] Log differentiating (6) we get:

$$\bar{M}' + \eta_m p'_m + m(Q^S/p_m)(\varepsilon_q w' - \Theta_k K') = 0. \qquad (6')$$

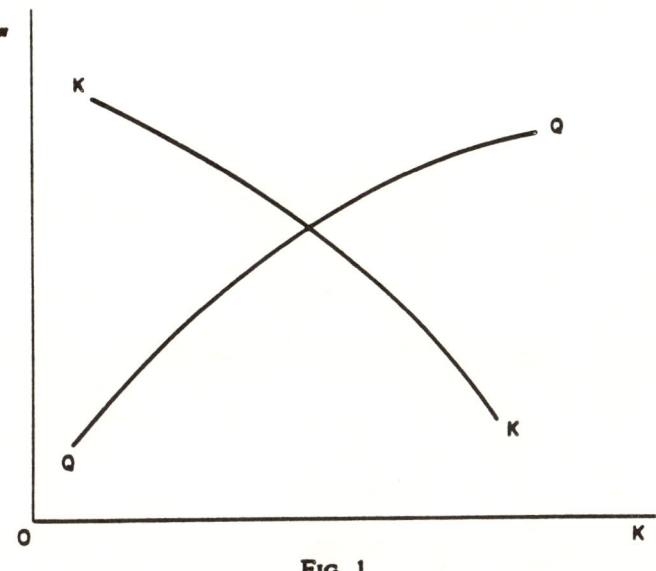

Fig. 1

where Θ_k is the supply elasticity of manufactures with respect to the stock of capital; q is the marginal propensity to consume domestic manufactures; η_q is the price elasticity of demand for domestic manufactures, defined positive; and ε_q is the price elasticity of the supply of domestic manufactures.

Since the marginal propensity to consume (q) is less than one,

$$\left.\frac{\partial w}{\partial K}\right|_{QQ} > 0,$$

as can be seen from the following argument: A rise in the capital stock raises output of manufactures but also income and hence demand. With a marginal propensity to consume local manufactures that is less than unity, however, there will be an excess supply. To restore equilibrium, the price of manufactures must decline. A price decline will restore equilibrium because, by raising real wages, it lowers output, income, and thus excess supply. At the same time, the price decline invites substitution away from imports to domestic goods, thus raising demand. Thus a high capital stock, in goods market equilibrium, leads to increased real wages and higher real income.[5]

---

[5] Using (3') and (5) we get: $dy/Q^s = [\eta_q/(1 - q)]w'$.

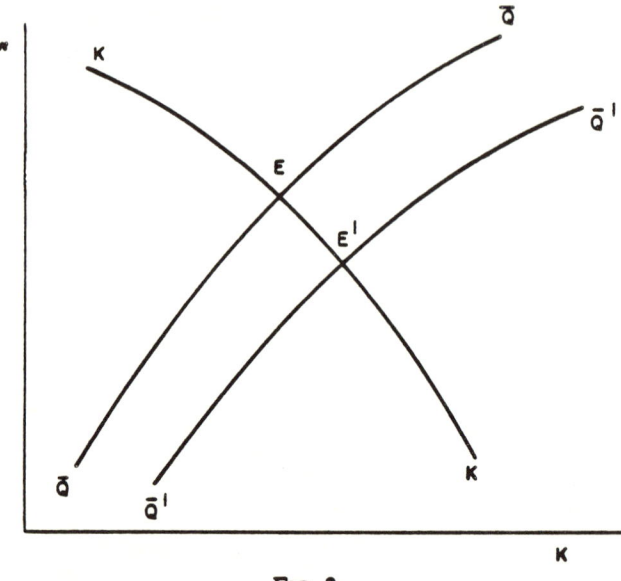

Fig. 2

The slope of $\dot{Q}\dot{Q}$ is interpreted as follows. If the capital stock rises, creating excess supply of home goods, this is eliminated through a fall in their price in relation to the price of the imported consumer good, that is, an increase in the real wage rate.

Observe that, as opposed to what occurred along QQ, the negative effect of the increase in the real wage rate on output completely eliminates the positive effect of the increase in the capital stock in such a way that income is constant along $\dot{Q}\dot{Q}$. This happens because, since the supply of imported goods is fixed by a quota, the excess supply of home manufactures induced by the increase in the capital stock has to be eliminated through a larger price effect than before. Equilibrium is determined at the point where $\dot{Q}\dot{Q}$ crosses KK.

The imposition of a stiffer import quota affects the system in the following way. To the extent that the government restricts the supply of imported manufactures, their price tends to rise. The increase in the price of competitive imports is accompanied by an increase in the

---

Substitution of (6') into (2') yields:

$$\varepsilon_q w' - \Theta_k K' - (\eta_q/\eta_m A)\bar{M}' = 0 , \qquad (7)$$

where $A = (1 - q) - m(\eta_q/\eta_m)(Q^S/p_m M)$.

demand for domestic manufactures. This substitution effect exerts upward pressure on the price of the latter, that is, it shifts $\dot{Q}\dot{Q}$ to the right.[9] As the price of the industrial home good goes up, the real wage rate falls. The rising rate of profits then fosters investment in the industrial sector, raising the equilibrium capital stock. At the new equilibrium (E' in fig. 2), the capital stock is higher and the real wage lower than before the stiffer import quota.

H. Exchange-Rate Devaluation

To understand the effect of a devaluation on the stock of capital, we begin by examining its consequences in the coffee market. Although a devaluation shrinks the dollar income of the coffee sector, because the demand for the product is inelastic in relation to its price, the income of the coffee sector measured in terms of the initial price of the domestic industrial product increases, because both the coffee output and the *cruzeiro* price of coffee go up.[10] This creates an excess demand for manufactures.

Furthermore, the demand for domestic manufactures expands to substitute for imported consumer goods which are now more expensive due to the devaluation. Given the capital stock, excess demand has to be eliminated through an increase in the price of the domestic good. This pushes real wages down, increasing the rate of profit and promoting additional investment. On the other hand, a devaluation increases the price of capital measured in terms of the domestic manufactured good, diminishing the rate of profit and depressing investment.

The final effect of a devaluation on the stock of capital is ambiguous as it responds to a positive stimulus, induced by excess demand on the home-goods market and to a negative stimulus, arising from the higher capital price.

The higher are the propensity to consume domestic goods and the price elasticity of their demand, the more will the demand for domestic manufactures expand in response to a devaluation and thus push up domestic prices, lower the real wage rate, and stimulate investment.

The lower is the share of capital in output, the less will the profit

---

[9] From (7) we have:

$$\frac{K'}{\bar{M}'} = -\left(\frac{\eta_q}{\theta_k \eta_m A}\right) < 0,$$

since $A > 0$. To show that $A > 0$, observe that $Q^D + p_m M + S = y$, where S = savings. By totally differentiating this expression we get $\eta_q(Q^S/p_m M) = \eta_m - 1$, which we substitute in A to obtain $A = [(1 - q - m) + 1/\eta_m] > 0$.

[10] From (1), the effect of a devaluation on the income of coffee measured in terms of the domestic manufactured goods is given by $(p_c C^S)' = \phi p'_m$, where $\phi = \eta_c(1 + \varepsilon_c)/(\varepsilon_c + \eta_c)$.

rate be affected by an increase in the price of the capital stock. Thus, a devaluation will increase the capital stock if the share of capital in industrial output is small and both the propensity to consume domestic manufactures and the price elasticity of demand for these goods are large.[11]

II. The Postwar Years

When quotas were lifted immediately after the war, imports climbed steeply and created an external disequilibrium.[12] Since the demand for Brazilian main exports was not elastic in relation to their prices, their sales abroad could hardly have been promoted by exchange devaluations. In addition, the Brazilian authorities feared that raising the price of imports by devaluing the national currency would push domestic prices up. It was therefore decided to correct the disequilibrium by establishing selective import controls. While this measure immediately reduced the deficit with countries having convertible currencies, it did not manage to stabilize domestic prices. The introduction of selective import controls also was associated with an acceleration of the industrialization process and a decrease in the relative importance of foreign consumer goods.

As demonstrated in Section I*H* quantitative restrictions on the importation of consumer goods have a positive effect on capital accumulation. In the first place, when less goods are imported, the gap increases between their international price and their price to domestic consumers.[13]

In the second place, because an increase in the price of competitive imports raises the demand for domestic manufactures via the substi-

---

[11] The effect of a devaluation on the capital stock is calculated as follows: Taking into account the effect of a devaluation on income of the coffee sector, log differentiation of (2) yields $\varepsilon_q w' = -\Theta_k K' + Bp'_m = 0$, where $B = [\eta_q + q\phi(p_c C^S/Q^S)]/(1-q)$. From (4), $\Theta_L w' + \Theta_k K' + \Theta_L p'_L = 0$. Considering that $p'_m = p'_L$, since P^*_m and P^*_L are fixed, we can calculate:

$$\frac{K'}{p'_m} = \frac{1}{\varepsilon_q \eta_k + \Theta_k}\left(B - \varepsilon_q \frac{\Theta_k}{\Theta_L}\right).$$

Thus, $(K'/p'_m) > 0$ if $\Theta_L[\eta_q + q\phi(p_c C^S/Q^S)] - \Theta_k(1-q)\varepsilon_q > 0$.

[12] This arose from the fact that Brazil achieved trade surpluses with countries whose currencies were nonconvertible. At the same time, she imported much more than she exported to the United States and other countries with strong currencies. See Malan et al. (n. 1 above), pp. 142–49.

[13] Following the war, the increase in the domestic price of imported manufactures benefited not only the merchants who held import licenses (since the cost of obtaining them was more than offset by their market value), but also those government officials in charge of granting such licenses who engaged in corrupt practices (see Huddle, "Balanço de pagamentos e controle de câmbio no Brasil").

tution effect, it exerts upward pressure on the price of these manufactures. Between 1946 and 1952, the prices of industrial goods rose on average 8.4% per year.[14] Since production costs (wage and equipment prices) climbed more slowly than the prices of manufactures, the rate of profit rose and stimulated investment in the industrial sector. In the period 1945–52, the output of the sector grew by 92% and its stock of capital by 79%.[15] This growth is not attributable solely to changes in relative prices brought about by import controls. Even more important was the positive effect of external demand.

During World War II and up to July 1946, the U.S. Office of Price Administration maintained a ceiling on the price of coffee. This discouraged production and obliged Brazil to use her stocks, which, once depleted in 1949, contributed to the soaring coffee prices observed as of this year. Between 1949 and 1952, the external incentive was so strong that the price index for coffee exports doubled.

The favorable impact of higher export earnings on capital accumulation can be understood with the aid of the exercise in Section I.E. As export earnings rise, the demand for manufactures grows. Then, as the prices of the latter move upward, the rising profits encourage industrial investment.

This partly explains why the stock of capital expanded more rapidly in 1949–52 than in 1947–49. However, in 1948–49 the incentive to invest was to an extent offset by a rise in the prices of imported capital. This rise was due to changes in the dollar prices of foreign equipment, as well as to the general 40% increase in duties negotiated in Geneva in 1947. As shown in Section I.F, an increase in the price of imported equipment should diminish the stock of capital. Nevertheless, the changes in the prices of manufactures induced by the rise in those of competitive imports proved sufficient to guarantee positive net investments (though declining in 1948–49) over the period.[16]

We can therefore argue that the changes in relative prices enhanced the profitability of the manufacturing sector and encouraged industrial investment. This obliges us to reject—theoretically and empirically—Huddle's contention that the exchange policies and import restrictions lowered the rate of investment and the growth of product.

A final alternative that should be considered is the possibility of a devaluation, as proposed by Huddle. As demonstrated in Section I.H, the effect of a devaluation on the stock of capital is open to question since it may or may not have a positive impact on investment. Although Huddle is on weak grounds when criticizing Furtado, he is probably

---

[14] See Malan et al., p. 176, table III.18.
[15] See ibid., p. 321, table V.17.
[16] See ibid., p. 477, table A.III.6.

correct in questioning industrialization through discriminatory trade policies. It can be argued that the accelerated industrialization of the forties and fifties had a marked antiagricultural bias and therefore implied a weak long-range growth strategy. The trade policies of the Brazilian government in the immediate postwar period certainly were not optimal in this sense, even though they undoubtedly fostered the industrialization process of the country during the period.

CHAPTER IV

MINIDEVALUATIONS AND INDEXED WAGES :

The Brazilian Experience in the Seventies

1. Introduction

The importance of the expansion of the foreign sector to the economic growth of Brazil in the last decade has been repeatedly emphasized. In part, this expansion has been attributed to the utilization of minidevaluations since 1968.[1]

At the same time that it checked union activities and tightened wage controls, the military regime that assumed power in 1964 managed to gain the confidence of both Brazilian and foreign capitalists and increase government investments. Between 1968 and 1973, the official indexation and public-investment policies, aimed at maximizing growth while stabilizing the rate of inflation, coincided with a period of expansion of the international economy with respect not only to goods and services, but also to capital movements. The outcome was the so-called Brazilian 'miracle'.[2]

The model presented in this essay studies the sequelae of minidevaluations in the Brazilian economy. It also incorporates indexed wages and their interplay with minidevaluations, together with the effects these policies have on growth, inflation and the functional distribution of income.

Section 2 focuses on the external sector, and derives an equation for the behavior of the real exchange rate as a function of the inflation rate and the trade balance.

---

[1] See Fishlow (1974).
[2] See Bacha (1977) and Malan and Bonnelli (1977).

Section 3 describes the share of wages in output as a function of a wage-indexation policy and the bargaining power of wage earners vis-à-vis their employers.

Section 4 shows how the real growth rate of output is determined by the real exchange rate and the share of wages in output. It also brings in the link between money growth, inflation and the growth rate of output. These relationships combined with the real exchange rate and the wage share complete the model. We proceed from there to comparative dynamic exercises, illustrative of the recent behavior of the Brazilian economy.

Section 5 brings an exercise showing how an increase in the price of an imported input, as in 1974, accelerates inflation and decelerates growth.

Section 6 closes the essay with a discussion of the policies available for adjusting the Brazilian foreign accounts.

2. The trade balance and the indexed exchange rate

Domestic output, Q, uses an intermediate input, such as oil, in its production. The quantity of the imported input, N, is

$$N = nQ. \tag{1}$$

The supply of the imported input is infinitely elastic at the international dollar price p_n^*, and the demand for our exports is infinitely elastic at the international dollar price p_x^*. The *cruzeiro* price of our imports and exports are respectively: $p_n \equiv E p_n^*$ and $p_x \equiv E p_x^*$, where E stands for the nominal exchange rate, measured as the price of the dollar in *cruzeiros*.

Assuming $p_n^* \equiv p_x^* \equiv 1$, we define the real exchange rate as

$$\varepsilon \equiv E/p,$$

where p is the *cruzeiro* price of Q and K.

Output may be consumed domestically or transformed into an export good. Assuming that producers incur increasing costs of marketing abroad, we represent export supply as a function of output, where the proportionality factor is an increasing function of the real exchange rate

$$X = (h\varepsilon - A)Q, \tag{2}$$

A here is a parameter whose value varies inversely with technical progress in the transformation of the domestic output into an export good.

The real trade balance is

$$B = (h\varepsilon - A)Q - \varepsilon n Q. \tag{3}$$

Observe that $\partial B/\partial \varepsilon = \pi Q$, where $\pi = (h-n)$, and $\partial B/\partial \varepsilon < 0$ if $\pi > 0$. A drop in the real exchange rate will lead to an increase in both exports and the real cost of the intermediate input. Condition $\partial B/\partial \varepsilon < 0$ implies that the second effect is not strong enough to eliminate the positive trade balance allowed by the impact on exports of the devaluation of the real exchange rate.

Eq. (3) establishes that the trade balance will be in equilibrium if $\varepsilon = A/\pi \equiv \bar{\varepsilon}$.

Under a fixed exchange system, the nominal exchange rate, E, is set by the government. Since 1968, the Brazilian government has employed mini-devaluations, deciding about the frequency and magnitude of the devaluation taking into account their effect on the trade balance, together with their impact on the price level.

On the one hand, devaluations stimulate exports. On the other, they are inflationary because they raise import prices. This is soon reflected in the wholesale price index, reducing the impact of devaluations on exports. Due to such considerations, the Brazilian government does not attempt to completely eliminate the differential between internal and external inflation via adjustments of the nominal exchange rate, but it tries to make the real exchange rate approach the value $\bar{\varepsilon}$, for which the trade balance is in equilibrium.

For our purposes, the devaluation formula can be expressed as

$$E' = \rho p' + \mu(\bar{\varepsilon} - \varepsilon), \qquad \rho < 1. \tag{4}$$

An apostrophe indicates a logarithmic derivative relative to time, i.e., $x' = (dx/dt)/x$.

From (4), the rate of change of the real exchange rate is

$$\varepsilon' = (\rho - 1)p' + \mu(\bar{\varepsilon} - \varepsilon). \tag{5}$$

Thus, changes in the real exchange rate are inversely related to the rate of inflation.

3. Indexed wages

We assume the existence of labor-augmenting technical progress. The quantity of effective labor, H, and real employment, L (hours worked), are given, respectively by

$$H = lQ, \tag{6}$$

$$L = le^{-\beta t}Q, \tag{7}$$

where β is the rate of labor-augmenting technical progress.

The nominal wage per hour worked is $W = U e^{\beta t}$, where U stands for the wage paid to effective labor.

Minimum wages have been indexed according to an official formula which takes into account only part of the rises in the price level and productivity gains:

$$W'_m = \lambda p' + \xi \beta, \qquad 0 < \lambda < 1, \quad 0 < \xi < 1,$$

where W'_m is the growth rate of the minimum wage.

Market wages are assumed to fluctuate around the minimum wage, depending on the bargaining power of wage earners vis-à-vis their employers. However, there is a limit to the wage increases that can be obtained by the working class. According to Marshall (1930), a ceiling on wage bargaining is imposed by the need to maintain a supply of capital and business power in industry. Arguing along the same lines, Kaldor (1960) points to the fact that the share of profits cannot fall below the level which yields the minimum profit rate capable of encouraging capitalists to invest.

Let us assume that the real share of wages (ω) approaches the ceiling (ψ) in accordance with a rate of adjustment determined by the bargaining power of the wage earners.

Therefore,

$$W' = \lambda p' + \xi \beta + \gamma(\psi - \omega).$$

The share of wages in gross output at market prices, ω, is $(LW)/(pQ)$. From (7), $L' - Q' = \beta$. It follows that the rate of change of the share of wages in output is

$$\omega' = W' - p' - \beta = (\lambda - 1)p' + (\xi - 1)\beta + \gamma(\psi - \omega), \qquad (8)$$

where $\lambda < 1$, $\xi < 1$ and $0 < \gamma < 1$.

4. The real growth rate and inflation

Value added is defined as gross output less the real costs of the imported input,

$$Y = Q - \varepsilon N = (1 - \varepsilon n)Q,$$

where $(1 - \varepsilon n) \equiv \alpha$ is the real value added per unit of putput.

Thus, the value added production function is

$$Y = \alpha Q. \qquad (9)$$

Formula (10) relates unit value added at factor cost, Z, and market prices

$$p = (1/1-\tau)Z, \qquad (10)$$

where τ is the tax rate.

Nominal profits equal value added less the wage bill. Thus, real profits are $[(1-\tau)\alpha Q - (W/p)L]$.

Real savings, S, are determined by the fraction s of real profits which is saved, plus the real trade deficit, plus the share of capital goods, ϕ, in government expenditures.[3] Hence,

$$S = s[(1-\tau)\alpha Q - (W/p)L] - B + \phi G. \qquad (11)$$

Investment is explained by the simple accelerator model, which argued that the rate of investment is proportional to the changes in output,

$$I = (1/a)(dQ/dt). \qquad (12)$$

Equality between savings and investment implies

$$dQ/dt = a\{s[(1-\tau)\alpha Q - (W/p)L] - B + \phi G\}.$$

Dividing the above expression by Q, we obtain the growth rate of real output,

$$Q' = a\{s[(1-\tau)\alpha - \omega] - b + \phi g\}, \qquad (13)$$

where $g \equiv G/Q$ and $b \equiv \pi \varepsilon - A$.

From (13), it can be readily seen that the growth rate of output is a declining function of the share of wages in output and of the real exchange rate. If the share of wages in output increases, private saving decreases and

---

[3]Observe that savings are made of that part of output which is not consumed,

$$S = Q - C - X - (1-\phi)G,$$

$$S = Q - \frac{WL}{p} - (1-s)\left[(1-\tau)\alpha Q - \frac{WL}{p}\right] - X - (1-\phi)G.$$

Note that $\alpha = 1 - en$; hence

$$S = s\left[(1-\tau)\alpha Q - \frac{WL}{p}\right] + [\varepsilon n Q - X] + \phi G + (\tau \alpha Q - G).$$

If the government budget is balanced, then: $\tau \alpha Q = G$ and the above expression reduces to (11).

growth decelerates: $\partial Q'/\partial \omega = -as$. If the real exchange rate rises, the cost of intermediate inputs also rises, thereby lowering profits and consequently reducing internal savings. On the other hand, when the exchange rate is devalued, the trade deficit (i.e., external savings) diminishes:

$$\partial Q'/\partial \varepsilon = -a[s(1-\tau)n + \pi].$$

We now turn to the money market. Assuming that the government can control the monetary base and that the bank multiplier is constant, the rate of growth of the money supply may be held to be determined by the government and to be equal to M'. Assuming a constant velocity, the rate of inflation equals the money growth rate minus the rate of growth of output,

$$p' = M' - Q'. \tag{14}$$

Eqs. (14), (13), (5) and (8) describe our economy. Substituting (13) into (14) and the expression for the inflation rate thus obtained into (5) and (8) yields

$$\varepsilon' = M' - a\{s[(1-\tau)\alpha - \omega] - b + \phi g\} - \Phi_1(\bar{\varepsilon} - \varepsilon), \tag{15}$$

$$\omega' = M' - a\{s[(1-\tau)\alpha - \omega] - b + \phi g\} + \Phi_3 \beta - \Phi_2(\psi - \omega), \tag{16}$$

where

$$\Phi_1 = \mu/(1-\rho),$$

$$\Phi_2 = \gamma/(1-\lambda),$$

$$\Phi_3 = (1-\xi)/(1-\lambda).$$

Eqs. (15) and (16) form the core of our analysis. They set the relative prices in the economy, i.e., the real exchange rate and the real wage rate. These, in turn, due to their influence on private savings and on the trade balance determine real growth and the inflation rate.

Solution of the system formed by (15) and (16) is illustrated in fig. 1.[4]

---

[4]Observe that

$$\left.\frac{\partial \varepsilon}{\partial \omega}\right|_{\varepsilon'=0} = -\frac{as}{J+\phi_1}, \tag{17}$$

and

$$\left.\frac{\partial \varepsilon}{\partial \omega}\right|_{\omega'=0} = -\frac{as\Phi_2}{J}, \tag{18}$$

where $J = a[s(1-\tau)n + \pi]$.

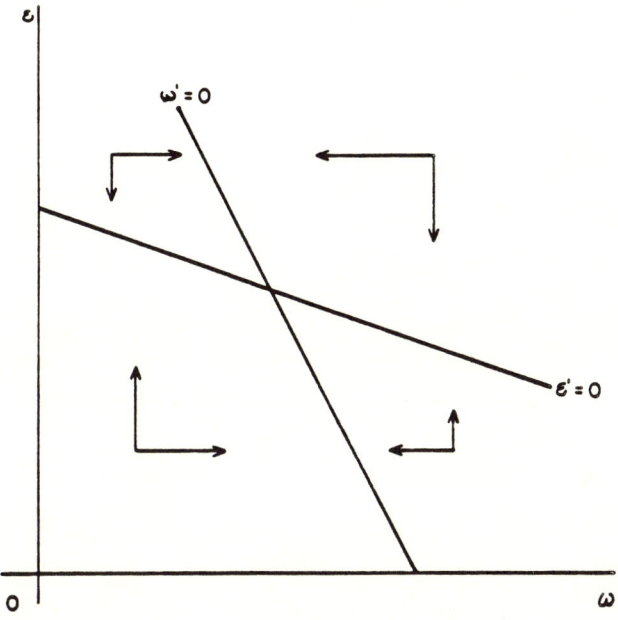

Fig. 1

Assume that the real exchange rate and the share of wages in output lie on the $\varepsilon'=0$ schedule. If ω increases, this reduces private savings and growth. Since the growth rate of money is given, inflation rises pushing down the real exchange rate.

Assume that the real exchange rate and the share of wages in output lie on the $\omega'=0$ schedule. If ε increases, this reduces both private savings and foreign savings and thus the real growth rate falls. Once money growth is given, inflation goes up reducing the real wage rate and the share of wages in output.

Inspection of (17) and (18) immediately reveals that the $\varepsilon'=0$ schedule is flatter than the $\omega'=0$ schedule, as required for stability and illustrated in fig. 1.

In the context of this less than fully indexed economy, policy-makers can affect growth in different ways.

(i) If the money growth rate increases, the public adds the money created by government to their cash balances only at higher rates of inflation. As the inflation rate rises, on one hand, the share of wages in output

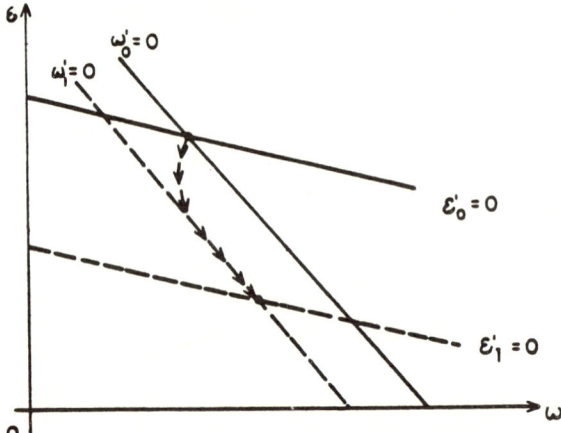

Fig. 2. An increase in autonomous exports.

falls, expanding private savings. On the other hand, the real exchange rate appreciates reducing the cost of intermediates, and augmenting the trade deficit. All these effects contribute to an increase in the real growth rate. Thus it is possible to achieve higher growth rates at higher rates of inflation, but at the cost of a decreasing share of wages in output and increasing trade deficits.[5]

(ii) A reduction in the share of productivity gains received by wage earners raises both private savings and the real growth rate. If the growth rate of the money supply is fixed, the rate of inflation falls. If the exchange rate is not perfectly indexed, the drop in the rate of inflation raises the real exchange rate over time, and the trade balance improves. This improvement, in turn, lowers, external savings, thus dampening (but not canceling) the impact of the decrease in the share of wages in output on

---

[5]An increase in the money growth rate shifts both $\varepsilon'=0$ and $\omega'=0$ to the left. Effects on the share of wages in output, the real exchange rate, the inflation rate and real growth are given by

$$d\omega = (\Phi_1/\Delta)dM' < 0,$$
$$d\varepsilon = (\Phi_2/\Delta)dM' < 0,$$
$$dp' = -(\Phi_1\Phi_2/\Delta)dM' < 1,$$
$$dQ' = dM' - dp' < 0,$$

where

$$\Phi_1 = \mu/(1-\rho), \quad \Phi_2 = \gamma/(1-\lambda), \quad \Delta = -[\Phi_1(as+\Phi_2)+J\Phi_2] < 0.$$

real growth and inflation.[6]

(iii) An increase in the share of capital goods expenditures in total public outlays pushes up growth and reduces the inflation rate. As the inflation rate falls, both the share of wages in output and the real exchange rate increase, savings are reduced, thus dampening but not offsetting the positive effect on growth of the larger capital accumulation by the government.[7]

(iv) An increase in public expenditures financed through taxes increases growth and reduces the inflation rate, as long as the capital goods share in total public outlays is larger than the marginal propensity to save of capitalists, i.e., $\phi > s$.[8]

In what follows we relate the above exercises to Brazilian economic growth.

5. Notes on the recent Brazilian experience

Comparative dynamics exercises in the last section confirmed that the government can lower the rate of inflation while accelerating real growth by diminishing the share of wage earners in productivity gains, by raising the share of capital goods expenditures in total public outlays, and by financing higher public expenditures through taxes (when $\phi > s$).

---

[6] A decrease in the share of productivity gains by wage earners $(-d\xi)$ shifts $\omega' = 0$ to the left. Effects on the share of wages in output, the real exchange rate, the inflation rate and real growth are given by

$$d\omega = -[[J+\Phi_1][\beta/(1-\lambda)]/\Delta](-d\xi) < 0 \quad \text{since} \quad \Delta < 0,$$

$$d\varepsilon = \frac{as[\beta/(1-\lambda)]}{\Delta}(-d\xi) > 0,$$

$$dQ' = \frac{as\Phi_1\beta/(1-\lambda)}{\Delta}(-d\xi) > 0,$$

$$dp' = -dQ' < 0,$$

where

$$J = a[s(1-\tau)n + \pi].$$

[7] The effect of an increase in the share of capital goods expenditures in total public outlays on the real growth rate is given by

$$dQ' = ag[-\Phi_1\Phi_2/\Delta]d\phi > 0 \quad \text{since} \quad \Delta < 0.$$

[8] This can be seen from

$$dQ' = a[-\Phi_1\Phi_2/\Delta][\phi - s]dg \quad \text{when} \quad dg = \alpha d\tau,$$

since $\Delta < 0$, $dQ' > 0$, if $\phi > s$.

Between 1968 and 1973, the twin goals of government policy were to step up the growth rate of product and to steady the rate of inflation by carrying out the three above-mentioned policies, while expanding the money supply. Consequently, capital growth was pushed up by public investments and private savings. The government share of the increase in this rate contributed relatively more, and private savings relatively less, to the growth rate of capital stock.

Thanks to the trust that capitalists placed in the government and to the ease of maneuvering allowed by the suspension of democracy, the Brazilian authorities were able both to increase the government share in the capital stock and to reduce the share of workers in productivity gains, keeping profits at a high level. Adherence to these policies led to public enterprises gaining unprecedented importance in the economy. While capitalists profits were assured, their power base was eroded.

There was no deliberate pressure against the capitalists as shown by a rising profit rate and a working class being squeezed. Nonetheless, at the political level, the outcome of these strategies was an anti-government coalition comprised of the most diverse strata of public opinion: workers protested that they were being deprived of the benefits of growth, and entrepreneurs that they were being stripped of the power, conferred by the ownership and control of the means of production.

Clearly, the performance of the Brazilian economy in the years 1968–1973 cannot be solely ascribed to government policies aimed at stepping up the growth rate. It was also due to an exceptionally favorable development of the world economy. The auspicious world situation brought an increase in the autonomous Brazilian exports of goods and services. [In the model, this increase is represented by a drop in A in eq. (2).]

The increase in autonomous exports acts on growth and distribution through its impact on the terms of trade. If autonomous exports expand, the exchange rate that balances the trade account declines. As the exchange rate appreciates, the reduction in the cost of intermediate imports enhances private savings. As a consequence, both investment and the growth rate of output increase and the inflation rate falls, permitting a slight improvement in the share of wages in output. This dampens the positive effect of the appreciation of the exchange rate but does not completely offset it.[9]

---

[9]An increase in autonomous exports $(-dA)$ is represented in fig. 2. Its effects on the share of wages in output, the real exchange rate, and growth are given by

$$d\omega = \frac{1}{\Delta} \cdot \frac{\Phi_1}{\pi} \cdot a[s(1-\tau)n + \pi(1-s)] \cdot (-dA) > 0,$$

$$d\varepsilon = -\frac{1}{\Delta} \cdot \frac{\Phi_1}{\pi} \left[as + \Phi_2 + as\frac{\Phi_2}{\Phi_1}\pi \right](-dA),$$

$$dQ' = -((1-J)as\Phi_2 + (1-as)as\Phi_1 + (J/\pi - as)\Phi_1\Phi_2)/\Delta$$

$dQ' > 0$ since $J < 1$, $as < 1$, and $as < J/\pi$.

The marked discontinuity observed in the development of the Brazilian economy in 1974 was in great part owing to the reversal of the world economy. The most important phenomenon in this reversal was the steep rise in oil prices. An increase in the price of the imported intermediate input can be understood as a reduction in domestic productivity.[10] Its main impact comes through a deterioration of the terms of trade. Higher production costs of the domestic good reduces savings and the result is stagflation: less growth and more inflation. Since wages are not perfectly indexed, the functional distribution of income deteriorates. The decrease in the share of wages in output leads to the oil crisis generating distribution problems that transcend the problem of administering the balance of payments.

6. Inflation, growth and the external debt

Up to now we implicitly assumed that the Brazilian economy does not find difficulties in financing a lasting trade deficit, and thus can support part of its growth through foreign savings.

The persistence of a trade deficit, year after year, implies that the external debt of the country is climbing. As a matter of fact, over the period 1973–1976, Brazilian gross-external debt more than doubled from 12.5 to 26.0 billion dollars. The debt/GDP ratio went from 8 to 14 percent.

There is growing uneasiness concerning the economic and political costs of the growing external debt. Some economists have argued that the exchange rate is too high, and that the government should 'maxidevalue' the cruzeiro in order to adjust the country's external accounts.[11]

In the model, 'maxidevaluation' is equivalent to a jump in the exchange rate as illustrated in fig. 3. Its first effect is to raise the production costs of the domestic good, thereby reducing value added and consequently diminishing private savings. This means that, at the previous real wage rate, the real growth rate is necessarily lower. The fact that the rate of growth falls while the growth rate of the money supply remains unchanged implies that

---

[10] A fall in productivity can be seen as a rise in the imported input/output ratio, shifting both $\omega' = 0$ and $\varepsilon' = 0$ upwards.

Effects on main variables are

$$d\omega = \frac{1}{\Delta}\left[\Phi_1 as(1-\tau)\left(\frac{n}{\pi}+1\right)\right]\varepsilon\, dn < 0,$$

$$d\varepsilon = -\frac{1}{\Delta}\left[\Phi_2[1-as(1-\tau)]+\frac{\Phi_1}{\pi}(as+\Phi_2)\right]\varepsilon\, dn > 0,$$

$$dQ' = \frac{1}{\Delta}\left[\Phi_1\Phi_2 as(1-\tau)\left(\frac{n}{\pi}+1\right)\right]\varepsilon\, dn < 0.$$

[11] See Pastore et al. (1976).

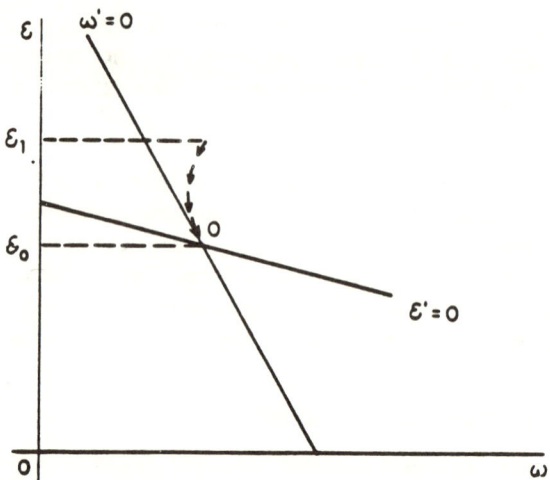

Fig. 3. A 'maxidevaluation'.

the inflation rate should increase. Since exchange rate and wages are not fully indexed, both the real exchange rate and the share of wages in output fall. However, as the share of wages in output and the real exchange rate diminish, savings over time recovers, until the initial impact on the trade balance, growth and inflation disappears.

Alternatives to correct the external accounts would be:

(i) A reduction of the growth rate of the money supply.

A lower money growth rate brings about a drop in the inflation rate and a consequent rise of both the real wage and the real exchange rate. As the exchange rate diminishes, the trade deficit shrinks, as wanted, but the cost of intermediate inputs goes up, savings are reduced and growth decelerates. The increase in the share of wages in output also reduces growth.

(ii) An acceleration of minidevaluations.

An increase in the exchange rate adjustment factor ρ causes the real exchange rate to depreciate inducing an improvement in the trade balance, higher *cruzeiro* prices of intermediate goods, less growth and more inflation. Higher inflation rates reduce the share of wages in output, dampening but not cancelling the negative effects of the higher real exchange rate on growth.[12]

Note that all policies for correcting the trade deficit, imply on lower growth rates. To avoid this, the economy would have to become less dependent on imported inputs.

References

Bacha, E., 1977, Issues and evidence on recent Brazilian economic growth, World Development 5 (1-2), Jan., Feb., 47-68.
Fishlow, A., 1974, Indexing Brazilian style: Inflation without tears?, Brookings Papers on Economic Activity 1, 261-282.
Kaldor, N., 1960, Alternative theories of distribution, in: Essays on Value and Distribution (G. Duckworth, London).
Malan, P. and R. Bonnelli, 1977, The Brazilian economy in the seventies: Old and new developments, World Development 5 (1-2), Jan., Feb., 19-46.
Marshall, A., 1930, Principles of economics, 8th ed. (Macmillan, London).
Pastore, A. C. et al., 1976, A teoria da paridade do poder de compra, minidesvalorizações e o equilíbrio da balança comercial Brasileira, Pesquisa e Planejamento Econômico 6, no. 2, Aug., 287-312.

---

[12]The $\varepsilon'=0$ schedule rotates upward for an increase in the exchange rate adjustment factor. ρ. Consequently the real exchange rate increases and the share of wages in output falls

$$d\varepsilon = -\frac{[as+\Phi_2]\Phi_1\left(\frac{\bar{\varepsilon}-\varepsilon}{1-\rho}\right)}{\Delta}\rho > 0,$$

$$d\omega = \frac{J\Phi_1\left(\frac{\bar{\varepsilon}-\varepsilon}{1-\rho}\right)}{\Delta}\rho < 0.$$

The effect on growth is

$$dQ' = (J\Phi_2\Phi_1[(\bar{\varepsilon}-\varepsilon)/(1-\rho)]/\Delta)\rho < 0 \quad \text{since} \quad \Delta < 0.$$

PART II

STABILIZATION EXPERIENCE IN LATIN AMERICA

CHAPTER V

STABILIZATION IN LATIN AMERICA:

POPULAR MODELS AND UNHAPPY EXPERIENCES

1. Introduction

High inflation rates and balance of payment crises are the everyday experience of Latin Americans. Stabilization policies that cut down on growth performance, the inevitable medicine.

Figure 1 shows the annual growth and inflation rates in Latin America between 1970 and 1984. Contrary to what one would predict from Phillips curves trade-offs, inflation and growth have a negative correlation. There is a good reason why. In the seventies, with plentiful external credit, Latin America experienced fast growth and relatively low inflation until faced with a balance of payments crisis in the early eighties. To cut on imports and promote exports, governments then reduced growth and devalued the exchange rate. But devaluations are inflationary. Thus, policies designed to restore external balance ultimately gave little help with growth but always led to more inflation.

One could further argue that growth, previous to the stabilization programs, was in good measure induced by large budget deficits financed by

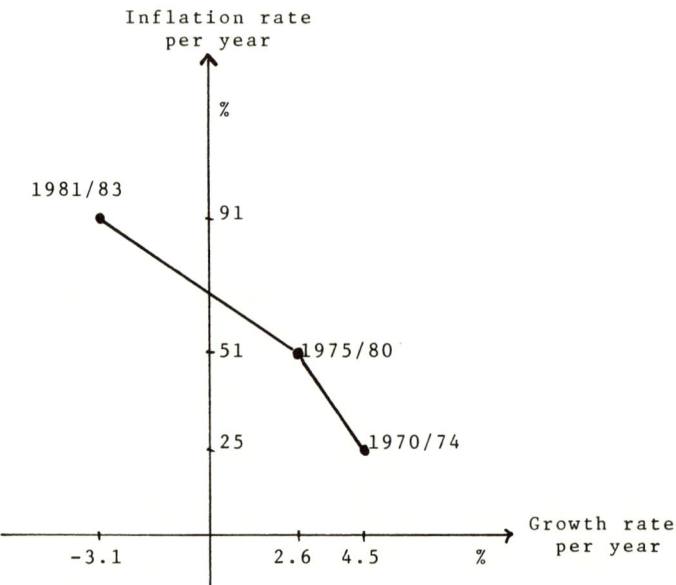

FIGURE 1
INFLATION AND GROWTH IN LATIN AMERICA, 1970/83

Source: CEPAL, Balance Preliminar de la Economia Latino-
americana, Dec. 1984.

external borrowing. Governments might not have succeeded in cutting those deficits during the period that followed the balance of payments crisis and being unable to obtain foreign resources, they resorted to forced savings through the collection of an increased inflation tax.

The arguments above explain why periods of growth and low inflation occur at the same time as trade deficits and abundant external credit. Periods of contraction in growth and high inflation, by contrast, coincide with external credit rationning and trade surplusses, as shown in Table 1.

TABLE 1

LATIN AMERICA MACRO INDICATORS, 1979/84

Averages per year

Indicator	1979-81	1982-84
GDP% per capita	2.1	-2.8
Inflation %	55.8	126.9
Trade surplus in U$ billions	-1.1	26.2

Source: CEPAL, Balance Preliminar de la Economia Latinoamericana durante 1984, mimeo, 1984.

The interpretations of such facts are not necessarily exclusive, although different models and different schools of thought emphasize different aspects of the same problem. Economists of a more conservative strand tend to believe that adjustments costs are short-lived. Once budgets are cut and devaluations have restored relative prices to their right levels, the economy adjusts quickly and growth resumes.

Others would emphasize that economies take time to adjust in response to changes in relative prices and that in the meantime wage earners bear most of the burden of adjustment. Both theory and history had demonstrated how real wage cuts restore external equilibrium and provide for the bulk of forced savings that finance the budget deficit. During a stabilization program à la IMF, wage earners have to live with more unemployment and lower real wages until capital moves to the traded goods sector, which becomes more profitable thanks to the exchange rate devaluations. Until then, falling standards of living and political unrest become an important ingredient of such experiments.

This paper surveys popular models of economic stabilization in developing countries, used over the past three decades. Much of the thought and experience during the fifties and sixties relied on Meade (1951), and Swan-Mundell internal-external balance. A model of internal and external equilibrium is described in the second section and then used to discuss the implications of orthodox programs.

The experience during the seventies diverge from earlier ones because of the greater importance of capital movements. A model based on Dornbusch (1980, 1982) and Rodriguez (1982) is presented in the third section. A discussion of recent programs and of the balance of payments crisis of the eighties then follows.

The recessions induced by high real interest rates in Latin America makes one suspicious of the "repressed economy" models. The fifth section briefly discusses their theoretical and empirical problems.

A survey of popular models in Latin America would not be complete before the structuralist school is taken into account. That discussion concludes the paper.

2. Orthodoxy

The models made popular in the fifties emphasize competitivenesses, inflation and budget deficits. Examining internal and external equilibrium they focus our attention on three variables: the real wage rate, w-e, the real money stock, h-e, and the share of the budget deficit in full employment output, f. The real wage rate is defined as $w-e \equiv \log(W/EW^*)$, and it is assumed that the price of domestic goods are equal to the domestic wage rate, while the foreign wage equals foreign prices, which are assumed to be constant and equal to 1. Lower case letters represent logarithms. The real wage rate, w-e, can thus be taken as the inverse of the real exchange rate and interpreted as a measure of our competitiveness in world markets. Along the same lines, the real money stock is defined as $h-e \equiv \log(H/EW^*)$. The use of foreign prices as our numéraire makes the algebra simple. Results can be easily extended to more complicated specifications, as pointed out in footnote 3.

Demand for output is assumed to depend positively on the budget deficit and on real cash balances, and inversely on the real wage, since an increase in real wages reduces our competitiveness abroad and diverts demand from domestic goods towards foreign goods. Given the budget deficit, combinations of the real wage and of the real money stock such that demand for output equals its potential level can be represented by an upward sloping schedule[1] like y = 0 in figure 2:

(1) $y(w-e, h-e, f) = 0$

---

1. The output gap is defined as $y \equiv \log(Y/\bar{Y})$, where Y and $\bar{Y}$ represent respectively current and potential output.

One can immediately verify that points to the left of y = 0 represent situations of unemployment.

We show external equilibrium in figure 2 along the schedule B = 0, having assumed that the current account improves with reductions of either the real wage or the real balances or the fiscal deficit:

(2) $\qquad B(w-e, h-e, f) = 0$

Points to the right of the schedule B = 0 represent current account deficits and points to the left, current account surplusses. At point E, the economy enjoys full employment and current account equilibrium, while its private sector pays the inflation tax that finances the budget deficit. We call the steady state inflation rate π and we define steady state velocity, or the ratio of potential output to the real money stock as v. We can thus write:

(3) $\qquad \pi = vf$

Point A in figure 2 represents an economy suffering from unemployment and a current account deficit. To know whether it can rest at point A or is moving somewhere else, we need to find out the dynamics controlling the real wage rate and the real money stock.

We first look at the dynamics of the real money stock, which depends on the behavior of the nominal stock and on the behavior of the nominal exchange rate. Changes in the nominal money stock are determined by domestic credit creation used to finance the budget deficit and by changes in foreign reserves. We write the expression for changes in the money stock as time goes by as $\dot{H}$. It is a function of the budget deficit, F, and the current account surplus, B, that is: $\dot{H} = (F+B) \cdot EW^*$. We then divide both sides of

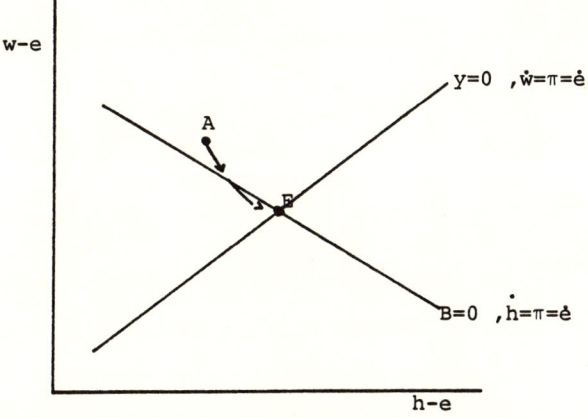

Figure 2

this equation by H, and we divide and multiply the right hand side by $\bar{Y}$. Having defined velocity and the shares of the budget deficit and of the current account surplus in output respectively as v, f and b, we can write[2] the expression for the growth rate of the nominal money stock as:

(4) $$\dot{h} = (f+b) \cdot v$$

To specify the behavior of the real money stock we still have to find out what determines the nominal exchange rate. Before we do that, we look at the behavior of wages.

The wage inflation rate exceeds trend inflation whenever demand for output exceeds its full employment level:

(5) $$\dot{w} = \pi + ay$$

To determine the behavior of the real wage rate and of the real money stock, we must make explicit the government choice for the nominal exchange rate. We will make different assumptions and examine the possible outcomes. The assumption consistent with steady state equilibrium of zero unemployment and balanced current account is that $\dot{e} = \pi$. In that case, the real wage rate is constant along the y = 0 schedule and the real money stock is constant along the B = 0 schedule. Our economy could not rest at point A, but would be travelling in the direction of

---

2. Having specified that $\dot{h}=(f+b)\cdot\bar{Y}/(H/EW^*) = (f+b)\cdot v$, we should further observe that the real money stock, H/EW*, is equal to its demand, $L(Y,\dot{w},\dot{e})$, as required by equilibrium in the assets market. Thus velocity is not constant as assumed in (4), but a function of current income, and of changes in domestic and foreign prices. Footnote 3 will indicate how to extend the model to include a variable velocity term. Since our results are not reversed by the more realistic specification, we proceed under the simplistic assumption that velocity is constant.

point E, as shown by the arrows in³ figure 2.

Before we move on to new specifications, it is worth noting that as long as the current account is balanced, i.e., along the B = 0 schedule, the budget deficit is entirely financed by the inflation tax, that is, by forced domestic savings. To the right of the B = 0 schedule, the budget deficit is financed in part by foreign savings, i.e., by current account deficits. It is important to keep this point in mind. It helps understanding the facts described in the introduction. A reduction of foreign credit, that imposes a smaller current account deficit than the one faced before such constraint came into effect, will necessarily generate a higher inflation rate if the same budget deficit continues to exist.

We now explore the situation where the nominal exchange rate is fixed. As opposed to the previous story, if the exchange rate is kept fixed, that is, if $\dot{e} = 0$, the real money stock will be constant, that is, $\dot{h} = 0$, only if the budget deficit is entirely financed by a current account deficit. We represent this situation by a dashed schedule in figure 3.

On the other hand, the real wage will be constant if the unemployment rate is high enough, inducing cyclical deflation to compensate for the trend inflation. This would happen along the schedule $\dot{w} = 0$, in figure 3. At point A, there is unemployment, and the wage inflation is below its

---

3. We can extend the model by relaxing the hypothesis that velocity is constant and correctly defining the real money stock by dividing the nominal stock by the cost of living, which is a weighted average of domestic and foreign prices. Its inflation rate is given by: $\dot{q}=c\dot{w}+(1-c)\dot{e}$. The real money stock is constant as long as $\dot{h}-\dot{q}=(f+b)\cdot v(y,\dot{w},\dot{e}) - c\dot{w}-(1-c)\dot{e} = 0$. This equation can be represented by a schedule passing through point E and crossing the upward section of figure 2, where there is unemployment and current account deficits.

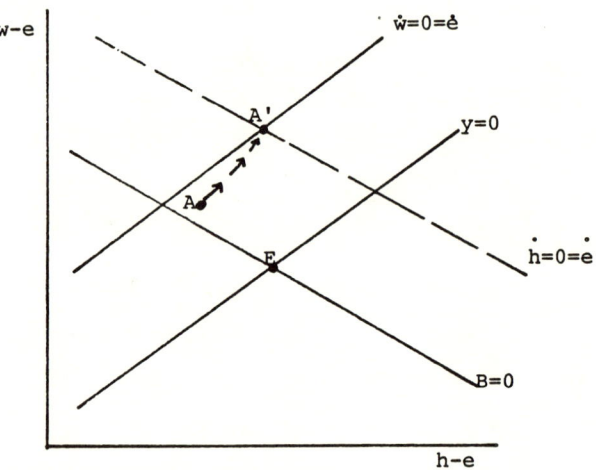

Figure 3

trend level π. But because it is still positive, it exceeds the zero devaluation rate. Thus, the real wage is increasing.

It is also the case that, at point A in figure 3, the budget deficit exceeds the current account deficit. Since domestic credit creation exceeds the reserves losses, the money stock is increasing. It follows that we are moving from A upwards in the direction of A', as indicated by the arrows in figure 3. Along the path AA', there is inflation and overvaluation, unemployment and a current account deficit. As long as the economy can borrow abroad to finance the external deficit, the inflation rate will be below the one that would prevail along $B = 0$, where the external balance is binding. At A', the situation of the balance of payments might be bad enough to force the government to devalue. In that case the economy would jump back to A, only to start once more its travel along the sad AA' path, with its never ending problems of inflation, unemployment, and increasing foreign debt.

The ageless orthodox medicine consists of two basic ingredients: a devaluation which reduces the real wage and the elimination of the budget deficit, which makes possible a steady state equilibrium with zero inflation. The travel in the direction to the new equilibrium will certainly involve unemployment. This result of course depends on the size of the devaluation, on elasticities and on how fast the economy adjusts to the change in relative prices. For most countries, the cuts in deficits and real wages is a sour medicine to swallow.

During the late 1950's Latin America suffered from the application of numerous orthodox programs: Chile (1956-58), Argentina (1959-62), Bolivia (1956), Peru (1959), and Uruguay (1959-62). The results were judged to be appalling. Temporary reductions in inflation and external deficits were combined with large increases in unemployment and a reduction of the labor share in output.

The Brazilian experience in the mid-sixties is often cited as a successful example of the program. Following several years of stagnation, high inflation and political unrest, the military coup of 1964 set a period of rigorous stabilization followed by years of prosperity. In the first period of the program, the budget deficit was drastically curtailed, by increasing taxes and reducing current government expenditures and at the same time expanding public investment. The exchange rate was devalued and restrictions on money wage increases were imposed as part of the program. As a result, the inflation rate fell to some 20% per year, which is modest by Brazilian and Latin American standards. Real growth at first fell, but after 1967 until 1973 it was kept around 10% per year, combined with a strong external position. The costs were not minor for the group who paid the bill. As Fishlow (1973), Macedo (1977) and Foxley (1981) show, real wages did fall during the stabilization program from their previous peak with bad effects for income distribution, only made possible by massive political repression.

There are other difficulties that one should be aware of. If nominal wages are indexed to past inflation rates, while the nominal exchange rate is kept fixed, rather than travelling directly to the new equilibrium, with lower real wages, we first take a detour up that could lead into a balance of payments crisis. In the Brazilian case, around 1968, policy makers realized that inflation was not about to disappear. To keep real wages at competitive levels, real appreciation of the exchange rate had to be avoided, which implied the adoption of a crawling peg. Chilean and Argentinian policy makers in the late seventies did not do the same and the results were the dramatic real appreciation of their currencies. We will discuss their problems in the next two sections.

In the meantime, there are important lessons to be derived from the model in this section and its malpractice. The first one is that the stabilization program has to be paid for. One must pay attention to the fact that, in the presence of real wage resistance, if prices are cost determined and mark-ups do not move, the cut in the budget deficit and in domestic credit creation, only induces more unemployment. As long as unemployment persists, the current account looks better, but its situation is not promising, since no structural change has taken place. This can be one of the reasons why IMF programs are unsuccessful in restoring growth and low inflation rates in countries assailed by balance of payments crisis. Another reason rests on the fact that even if those programs succeed in changing relative prices, adjustments in production in response to relative price changes might take long to come about. In the meantime, the income effects of the changes in relative prices will turn out hard to bear. Such costs were clearly an issue in the adjustment programs of the eighties, that we discuss later on.

3. Capital Mobility

Stabilization programs in the 70's have increasingly recognized the importance of capital mobility in the adjustment process. Since this problem turns around interest rates, the model in this section moves the analysis from real cash balances to the real interest rate, r, and accordingly modify equation (1). Demand for output is assumed to depend positively on the budget deficit and inversely on the real wage and on real interest rates, since an increase in the interest rate increases the opportunity cost of investment and reduces aggregate demand. Given the budget deficit, combinations of the real wage rate and the real interest rate such that demand for output equals its potential level can be represented by a downward sloping schedule like y = 0 in figure 4:

(6) $$y(w-e, r, f) = 0$$

Points to the right of y = 0 in figure 4 represent situations of unemployment.

We now look at interest rates determination. Perfect capital mobility implies that our nominal interest rate, i, equals the foreign interest rate, i*, adjusted for expected depreciation[4]:

(7) $$i = i^* + \dot{e}$$

We define the real interest rate as the difference between the nominal interest rate and the rate of inflation of the cost of living, $\dot{q}$, which is a weighted average of the inflation rates of domestic and imported goods: $\dot{q} = c\dot{w} + (1-c)\dot{e}$.

(8) $$r = i - (c\dot{w} + (1-c)\dot{e})$$

Substitution of (8) into (7), given the assumption of zero foreign inflation, yields:

(9) $$r = r^* + c(\dot{e}-\dot{w})$$

---

4. The framework of analysis is one of perfect foresight with respect to interest rates, inflation and depreciation.

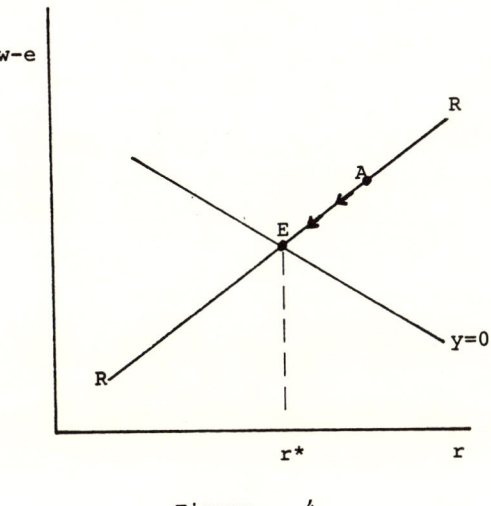

Figure 4

Equation (9) means that our real interest rate, adjusted for expected real appreciation equals foreign real interest rate.

We maintain the assumption that the wage inflation rate exceeds trend inflation whenever demand for output exceeds its full employment level (equation (5)).

As in the previous section, we will make different assumptions about the government choice for the exchange rate behavior. We start with the assumption consistent with steady state full employment equilibrium, i.e., $\dot{e} = \pi$. As before, if the depreciation rate equals trend inflation, real wages will be constant along the y=0 schedule.

We also want to represent assets market equilibrium in figure 4. This is done by substituting the devaluation rate, π, together with the wage inflation rate into (9):

$$(10) \qquad r = r^* - c \cdot y(w-e, r, f)$$

Equation (10) is represented by the schedule RR in figure 4. At point E, there is full employment, both the wage inflation and the depreciation rate equal trend inflation, and the domestic real interest rate equals the foreign one. At point A, in figure 4, there is unemployment and the wage inflation rate falls below trend inflation. There is real depreciation, and people only hold the stock of domestic bonds because it pays an interest rate higher than the foreign one. As the real wage falls, expected depreciation and domestic interest rates are reduced, and the economy travels in the direction of E.

For the moment, imagine that the economy is travelling from A in direction to E, and that the policy makers fix the exchange rate, making $\dot{e}=0$.

As shown in figure 5, once the nominal interest rate is fixed, the real wage rate is constant only if the unemployment rate is high enough, so that the cyclical deflation exactly compensates for trend inflation. This would happen along the schedule $\dot{w}=0$. On the other hand, the schedule representing assets market equilibrium shifts to the left, since domestic interest rates will only equal foreign ones when expected real depreciation is zero, which will now occur at point E'. As shown in figure 5, point A does no longer represent an equilibrium in the assets market. Since there is inflation, and the government has fixed the exchange rate, people now expect real appreciation and domestic interest rates fall. In figure 5, the economy jumps from A to A', and then, to E', as the real exchange rate appreciates domestic and real interest rates increase. The economy moves from A' to E', with falling inflation rates, but overvaluation. Consequently, unemployment increases and the current account deteriorates. When the economy reaches its zero inflation rate, the situation looks as dismal as the scientists responsible for the trick.

The movements of the real interest rate and the real wage described by the jump from A to A' and then by the movement in the direction of E' resembles the data for the same variables in Chile, between 1979 and 1981. Starting in 1965, the exchange rate regime in Chile has been one of minidevaluations designed to avoid abrupt changes of the real exchange rate, characteristic of periods when governments pursue inflationary finance. From 1978 until June 1979, Chile followed a tabular exchange rate regime. On June 30, 1979, the progression of the exchange rate table then in effect was interrupted and a fixed rate system was established.[5] As the model predicts, and Table 2

---

5. Rather than fixing the exchange rate at the previous level, the policy makers devalued to 39 pesos to the dollar and fixed at that level, at the same time as tariff rates were unified at 10 percent. The final effect was not a real devaluation. For a short but thorough history of trade and exchange rate policy in Chile, see Harberger (1982).

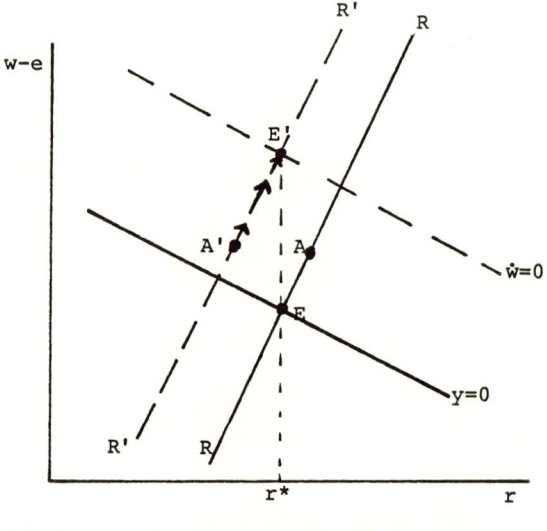

Figure 5

shows, the real interest rate falls in the second half of 1979 and then increases together with real wages. At the same time, unemployment increases and the current account deteriorates, while inflation converges to the international level.

TABLE 2

REAL INTEREST RATES AND REAL WAGE RATES IN CHILE

	1978	1979 1st	1979 2nd	1980	1981
Real interest rates % per month	2.99	1.79	0.83	1.05	2.75
Index of real wages 1970 = 1 (Univ. of Chile corrected CPI Deflator)	1.01	1.12		1.21	1.33 (June 1981)

Source: Real interest rates are interest rates charged for short term loans, Banco Central do Chile, Boletin Mensual, Julio 1982, p. 530. Real wage rates are from Harberger (1982), Table 6. The index for the real wage rate is .66 in 1975. Whatever the data used to calculate the real exchange rates in this period, one finds a clear real appreciation.

The recent stabilization program in Chile (1978-81) diverge from the previous ones by the fact that the dominant orthodoxy becomes the global monetarism of Johnson and Mundell, in which a fixed exchange rate is seen as the basic determinant of inflation, while fiscal discipline avoids undermining the program. Beyond that the task of the policy maker is to free markets. As the theory predicts, the inflation rate did converge to zero by 1981, but the overvaluation was enormous as well as the current account deficits.

The story told in figure 5 could be made more precise by the introduction of wage indexing, movements in foreign interest rates, government intervention in the assets market and fiscal reforms. We now explore the effects of an increase in foreign interest rates in the presence of real wage resistance. Real wages can be made rigid by the presence of indexation to the cost of living index, as represented by the horizontal schedule in figure 6. Constant real wages and assets market equilibrium now occur simultaneously at point A in figure 6. That is the point where the Brazilian economy sits around 1980, close to full employment, financing a large oil bill by foreign borrowing and suffering from high inflation rates. Under those circumstances, an increase in the foreign interest rate occurs. Assets market equilibrium can only be maintained if domestic interest rates also increase, as shown by point A' in figure 6. The increase in interest rates induces more unemployment. The trade balance improves, but the current account further deteriorates, with the increased interest payments on debt. The Brazilian policy makers, faced by a balance of payments crisis, further intervened in the assets market, increasing domestic interest rates above the international level, and thus creating the biggest recession the Brazilian economy has ever gone through in the post-war period. The fall in GNP in 1981 was estimated to be around 2%, in comparison with the trend growth of 7%, while inflation rates hardly moved. The balance of trade duly moved back into a surplus, but inflation increased and the recession persisted through 1983, while the authorities engaged in agreements with the IMF.

Other examples of unhappy stabilization programs during the 70's in Latin America are not lacking. Ramos (1980) gives a critical account of the Chilean experience after 1973. Foxley (1981) discusses the distributive effects of the programs in Chile (1973-78), Argentina (1976-78) and Uruguay

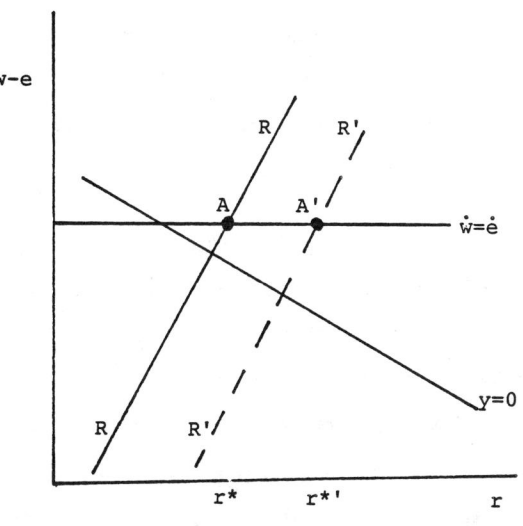

Figure 6

(1974-78). Diaz-Alejandro (1981) examines the vicious cycles between populism and dictatorship in the southern cone, paying special attention to capital movements in the seventies. Peru (1975-78) is discussed in Cline (1981) and Mexico (1977) in Weintraub (1981). Williamson (1982) compares the different strategies adopted in Argentina, Brazil, Chile and Colombia. This list is far from complete, but enough to support skepticism in relation to orthodox programs. Skepticism further increases when one looks at the stabilization experiments of the early eighties. We now turn to a comparison between the adjustment processes of the thirties and the eighties.

4. Two Major Latin American Depressions Compared

According to the IMF, thirty developing countries were in process of renegotiating their debts in 1983 and twenty Latin American countries were undergoing an adjustment program. The Economic Commission for Latin America (ECLA) reports that income per capita in L.A. fell by -3.3% in 1982 and -5.3% in 1983. In 1984 it increased by 0.2%, but it was still below its 1977 level. This large fall in income is in part attributed to the adjustment programs that took place in response to the contraction in international lending in 1982.

A striking fact of the seventies was the high growth rates of Latin American economies, despite the oil shock of 1973 and 1979, the recession in industralized economies in 1974/75 and 1980, and the many unsuccessful stabilization programs of the period. It looked as if Latin America had overcome the old external constraints. 1981 brought back the thirties nightmare. Tables 3 and 4 show real output per capita in Argentina, Brazil, Chile, Mexico and Peru, in the thirties and in the last two decades. In

1984, Chile and Peru were living with the same income per capita that they used to have twenty years ago. In Brazil, the depression in 1983 seemed deeper than in the thirties.

The facts that dominate the economic scenario in 1981/82, also resemble those before the Great Depression of the thirties: a fall in economic activity in the industrialized countries, a fall in the value of world trade, high interest rates, appreciation of the dollar and fall in the real price of commodities.

In 1929, economic activity in Latin America was dominated by international trade and the money supply was determined by international reserves movements. Policy makers were unable to control the sharp deflationary impact of both the adverse demand shock and the capital fights. Years would pass before the public outcry would become strong enough to revert the economic policies.

Thorp (1984) surveys the L.A. experience in the thirties. Recent interpretations support some of the old views held by the Economic Commission of Latin America (ECLA). In the ECLA interpretation, the consequences of the 29 crisis varied with the country's integration into the international system and the nature of her exports. In the case of tropical products, given the inelasticity of supply of perishable crops, the decline in demand provoked a large fall in prices. In the case of mineral products, the industrial slump in the importing countries led the collapse of production in the exporting countries, which, like Chile, were the hardest hit in L.A. The countries in the least vulnerable position were those exporting commodities with annual crop cycles, such as Argentina, specializing in temperate zone food products, with low income elasticities and better organized markets. Countries like Brazil, used to finance coffee surplusses, withdrawing them from the market, could also recover faster than others.

TABLE 3

INDICES OF REAL OUTPUT PER CAPITA

IN SOME L.A. COUNTRIES, 1929/33

Year	Argentina	Brazil	Chile	Mexico	Peru
1929	100.0	100.0	100.0	100.0	100.0
1930	93.5	93.6	92.0	91.2	87.2
1931	84.9	89.0	68.7	92.9	75.4
1932	80.1	89.4	67.2	76.5	70.3
1933	81.8	99.0	78.7	83.3	93.1

Sources: Banco Central de La Republica Argentina, Cuentas Nacionales: Series Historicas, vol. III, 1976; R. Zerkowski and M.A. Veloso, "Seis Décadas de Economia Brasileira através do PIB", Revista Brasileira de Economia, 36 (3), 1982; UN, Economic Survey of L.A., 1949, New York; 1951; CEPAL, Series Historicas del Crescimiento, Santiago: 1978; C. Bolona, "Estimaciones Preliminares del Producto Nacional", mimeo, Universidad del Pacifico.

Note: Statistics on population in the 30's for Peru were not available. Her population growth rate is estimated to have increased from 1.8% in the 40's to 3% in the 70's. To obtain the numbers in column 5 we assumed that the Peruvian population growth was 1.8% in the 30's.

TABLE 4

INDICES OF REAL INCOME PER CAPITA

IN SOME L.A. COUNTRIES: 1960/83

Year	Argentina	Brazil	Chile	Mexico	Peru
1960	79.3	44.0	72.7	49.0	72.1
1970	91.2	56.0	88.8	68.7	93.8
1979	100.0	95.8	90.7	90.0	98.8
1980	99.6	100.0	96.2	95.1	99.0
1981	92.5	94.2	100.0	100.0	100.0
1982	86.2	92.9	84.2	97.3	97.8
1983	87.4	87.9	82.1	89.8	84.8

Sources: IMF, International Financial Statistics, 1983, and CEPAL: Balance de la Economia Latino-Americana durante 1984.

The contraction of income provoked by the fall in exports was combined with capital flight and a reduction in the money supply. Those effects were worsened by the fact that policy makers tried to save the gold standard and enforced strong contractionary measures on their countries, as a first reaction to the crisis. In Argentina and Chile, for instance, credit was restricted and interest rates increased. In Argentina, real government spending only started to increase in 1935 when a program of massive road construction was implemented. In Chile the nominal exchange rate remained constant and the only significant anticyclical policy was an increase in 10% in real government production.

Peru suffered from the common balance of payments troubles but the effects were muted and short lived thanks both to default on the foreign debt in 1932, which doubled the import capacity overnight, and the fast recovery of export earnings. Thorp (1978) shows that half the coastal population in Peru earned their living from cotton and benefitted from the successful international price support scheme initiated in the United States to protect their farmers. The early revival of both cotton and petroleum exports were followed by a wave of reactivation of mining. Recovery in Peru thus was not linked to domestic fiscal and monetary policies. By contrast, in Peru and Colombia, government spending declined more rapidly than export earnings during the early depression years. In Peru, government expenditure fell by 50% between 1928 and 1931 with the interruption of external borrowing and was cut by another 32% in 1932, while taxes were increased to finance help for the unemployed. Only in 1936 public works began to expand.

Brazil provides an interesting example of compensatory expenditures. The key to understanding the behavior of the Brazilian economy in the

1930's is the coffee support policy, which held the income of the export sector at a high level and hence enabled the manufacturing sector to expand as the exchange rate was devalued.

As public protest against deflation mounted, most L.A. countries suspended normal servicing of the external debt and asked foreign creditors for reshceduling payments. The exchange rate was devalued, while exchange controls isolated the domestic economy from external pressures. The domestic credit expansion took the form of increased loans by the central banks to the government, to development institutions, to agricultural and mortgage banks and to various producers associations. Government spending also rose due to natural disasters, civil disturbances and border wars. Diaz-Alejandro (1983) points out the following examples: the war between Peru and Colombia over Leticia and the second Chaco war between Bolivia and Paraguay in 1932; the political turmoil in Chile during the socialist government of 1931/32; the São Paulo rebellion of 1932 and a severe drought in northeastern Brazil.

Recovery came about when real devaluations made import substituting activities profitable. In the mid thirties, real exchange rates in some L.A. countries were 70% higher than in the twenties. The fact that the Brazilian real exchange rate increased 43% between 1931 and 1929, at the same time as output per capita fell by 11%, is consistent with the hypothesis of small price elasticities in the short run. But pretty soon, the real devaluations would start to work, encouraging import substitution, while monetary and fiscal policies reversed from the initial contraction.

Cooper (1971) observes that although devaluations in L.A. are generally successful in improving the trade balance, they are not without political costs. In the thirties, the real devaluations were not obtained without popular turmoil. The period was characterized by increased social pressure, numerous strikes, the emergence of radical parties and nationalist rhetoric. Those were the years of Cardenismo in Mexico; the radical-socialist-communist "Popular Front" in Chile; Aprismo during its most revolutionary phase in Peru; the foundation of the Venezuelan Democratic Action Party; the peasant insurgency in El Salvador; and the "socializing" attempts in Bolivia and Equador.

Once workers get organized, real devaluations become more difficult to implement. During the fifties and sixties, many Latin American countries faced unsustainable current account deficits and tried to deal with the problem by devaluing their currencies. The typical program would consist of an attempt to tighten monetary policies coupled with major exchange rate devaluations. Between 1953 and 1963, that is, in ten years, a program of this type was implemented in five different times just in Brazil: by Getúlio Vargas in 1953/54, by Café Filho in 1954/55, by Juscelino Kubitscheck in 1958/59, by Jânio Quadros in 1961, and by João Goulart in the beginning of 1963. Everytime, the cost-push elements of the stabilization program (devaluations and gasoline price rises) accelerated inflation and induced social unrest forcing the program to be relinquished. Similar stories can be told for all Latin American countries.

The notorious case of successful stabilization is the Brazilian program in the mid-sixties that we discussed in the previous section. One of its legacies was the economy-wide indexation scheme that makes changes in relative prices almost impossible to obtain. The real exchange rate was kept constant during the seventies, even in face of external events that made the prevailing relative prices incompatible with sustainable current account deficits. Those deficits cumulated into the balance of payments crisis of 1982.

The 1982 balance of payments crisis in Latin America has been explained in part by the contraction of activity in the industralized countries. The recession hit the world trade in 1981. In 1982 international trade declined by 2%. The recession in industrial countries greatly reduced demand for commodities, while high real interest rates made the holding of stocks costly. As a consequence, non-fuel commodity prices fell. On the other hand, recession and rising unemployment in industrialized countries prompted an upsurge of protectionist pressure. The developed countries stepped up their restrictions against exports from developing countries, mainly by imposing import quotas or agreements to restrain exports. By 1981 most Latin American countries had run into serious balance of payments problems. While export revenues fell, high real interest rates increased their debt service obligations.

Dornbusch (1984) attributes the crisis to domestic mismanagement. Chile had moved to a fixed exchange rate, despite continuing inflation and indexation of wages. In Argentina, the external imbalance by early 1981 had been induced by the severe overvaluation, that was the legacy of unsuccessful attempts to use a preannounced exchange rate as an anti-inflationary device. The experiment started in December 1978 and left the country with severe current account deficits, a beginning recession and a large external debt. In 1981, repeated runs on the peso forced two large devaluations and the creation of a two-tier market. GDP continued to fall due to high interest rates. The external credit disruption associated with the Malvinas war added to the internal recession.

In Mexico, revenues from oil exports increased by 12 times from 1977 until 1981. However, in an attempt to speed up economic development government expenditures increased tremendously while public revenues lagged behind. To moderate inflation, increases in prices and tariffs of goods and services provided by the public sector were postponed and increased government deficits were financed by external borrowing. The effects of the international recession were significant both on oil sales and foreign debt service payments. The resulting current account deficits and the continuing deterioration of the balance of payments despite the 1981 and 1982 devaluations gave rise to the expectation that gradual depreciation of the exchange rate would be insufficient to correct the imbalances on current account. As a result, capital flight reached unprecedented levels. Their magnitude finally convinced the government to impose exchange controls, close the mexodollar market and nationalize the banking system.

After the emergence of the Mexican debt crisis in 1982, private credit, other than for trade financing, became virtually unobtainable on a voluntary basis for most developing countries. The abrupt slowing of credit commitments after a long period of rapid growth generated a serious concern — that the inability of some major borrowers to refinance maturing loans could precipitate a crisis of confidence in the solvency of the lending institutions themselves, and a major disaster for the whole network of international trade and payments. The threat that the borrowers could repudiate their debt set the IMF to save the system. By now, most Latin American countries have entered a system of IMF conditionality with a counterpart of bank financing of part of the foreign exchange gap.

Large devaluations and budget contractions were adopted in most Latin American countries. In Mexico, for instance, the critical target of the program called for a reduction of the public deficit from 17.6% of GDP in 1982 to 8.5% in 1983, while the exchange rate in the free market by January 1983 had depreciated by 5.6 times in relation to its level in

February 1982. By the end of 1983, most of the fears of financial disaster that pervailed one year before were banished. Large surplusses in the trade and current accounts were generated and the foreign debt renegotiated. The costs of adjustment were large. Approximately 750,000 jobs were lost and the results in the balance of payments were due mostly to a dramatic reduction in imports, while non-oil exports did not react as expected. Nonetheless, Mexico was held up as an example to other Latin American countries.

Real devaluations were large in most Latin American countries as shown in table 5, and contractionary policies were pervasive. By 1984, the results were considered impressive on the external side, where trade surplusses far exceeded expectations. But results were very negative as far as domestic performance is concerned. Growth turned negative and inflation increased.

TABLE 5

REAL EXCHANGE RATES IN L.A., 1975-1983

Period	Argentina	Brazil	Chile	Mexico	Peru
1975	100.0	100.0	100.0	100.0	100.0
1976/81	62.6	98.8	79.2	103.4	120.1
1982	99.6	97.8	85.1	131.7	137.8
1983		127.4	91.5	140.7	159.4

Sources: IMF, International Financial Statistics.

Note: The real exchange rate is defined as the ratio of the nominal exchange rate times U.S. wholesale prices divided by wholesale prices at home. In the case of Peru, wholesale prices were not available and consumer prices were used.

There are at least two elements responsible for the acceleration of inflation in the recent years. One is the cost push element of the stabilization program that reduces food and fuel subsidies, in order to balance the budget deficit. And the other one comes from the large devaluations.

In 1985, per capita income in Latin America although no longer falling remains as much as 10% below its pre-crisis levels. The terms of trade have not improved. The decline in debt/export ratios did not materialize. Inflation has risen, real wages have fallen and productive investment remains depressed. In September 1985, an earthquake in Mexico City prevented the Mexican president from attending the UN General Assembly in New York where he had been expected to make a forceful presentation on the debt issue. His case was bolstered by the argument that Mexico was facing new financial difficulties, even though until late 1984 its adherence to the IMF guidelines had been exhibited to other debtor countries as an example.

Experiments with orthodox programs in Latin America have been far from successful. The next section will claim that results to be obtained from the recommendations of the "repressed economy" model could be as bad.

5. The "Repressed" Economy

As opposed to the previous models, where high interest rates lead to protracted investment, unemployment and depressed growth, McKinnon (1973), Fry (1982) and others[6] have been able to produce a model where developing countries can induce more capital accumulation by increasing interest rates,

---

6. Fry (1982) surveys the literature on "repressed" economies and gives complete references to his own work.

and thus be reborn as free economies.

The essential elements of the "repressed" economy models consist on the following assumptions: Savings are an increasing function of the real interest rate. Nominal interest rate ceilings hold the real interest rate below the level at which savings and investment are equalized. Actual investment is limited to the amount of domestic savings. In the open economy, that proposition holds true, only if people cannot borrow abroad nor expand exports. The "repressed" economy is closely related to the two gaps model, in that it assumes investment to be determined by domestic and foreign savings. However, its empirical usefulness, as opposed to the two gaps model, is further limited by the central assumption of an interest responsive savings. That assumption is not verified empirically.

Leaving aside the government sector, we know from National Accounting that investment, I, is identically equal to savings, S, plus the current account deficit, measured in terms of our own good, $\varepsilon M - X$:

(11) $$I \equiv S + \varepsilon M - X$$

where the real exchange rate is defined as: $\varepsilon \equiv EP^*/P$.

Surplus labor exists and the aggregate supply function is:

(12) $$Y/K = \theta$$

It follows that output growth rate equals the growth rate of capital, I/K, called g. Assuming that imports are proportional to investment, $M = \alpha(\varepsilon)I$, with $\alpha' < 0$, we can write $\varepsilon M = m(\varepsilon)I$, where $m(\varepsilon) \equiv \varepsilon\alpha(\varepsilon)$. We further assume that the share of savings in income is a positive function of the real interest rate, $S/Y = s(r)$; and that the share of exports in output is a positive function of the real exchange rate, $X/Y = x(\varepsilon)$. We can thus rewrite (11) as:

(13) $$g = (\theta/1-m(\varepsilon))[s(r)-x(\varepsilon)] = \lambda(r,\varepsilon)$$

For a given real interest rate, r_o, we can represent equation (13) by a downward sloping schedule in figure 7.

By imposing the restriction that imports must equal exports we can derive a second expression for the growth rate from the current account:

(14) $$g = (\theta/m(\varepsilon))x(\varepsilon) = \phi(\varepsilon)$$

which we represent by the upward sloping schedule in figure 7. If the real exchange rate falls below ε_o, the growth rate determined by the current account is binding and we sit to the left of $g = \theta s(r_o)$, because at the going exchange rate we cannot afford to import the capital goods we need to grow faster. When the real exchange rate equals ε_o, both constraints are binding and the "repressed" economy grows at the rate $g = \theta s(r_o)$. Keeping the real interest rate constant and increasing the real exchange rate would do no good since we cannot grow by foreign machines alone, but also need the domestic investment (savings) to build the infrastructure for the machines to operate. A higher interest rate would shift the schedule $\lambda(r)$ to the right and, if combined with a higher real exchange rate, would induce faster growth.

To close the model, and explain why an increase in the nominal interest rate would induce both, higher real interest rate and higher real exchange rate, we have to explicit the mechanism that determines those variables. Both nominal interest rate and nominal exchange rates are determined by government, so all we must decide about is the behavior of domestic prices. Fry claims that this problem is solved by postulating

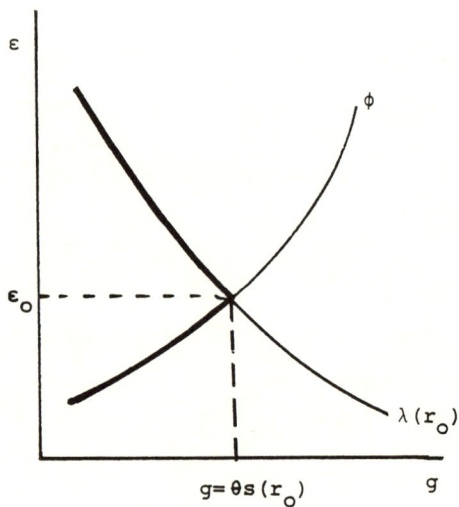

Figure 7

a Phillips curve. How to combine a full capacity model and zero current account deficit with a Phillips curve remains a mystery. In the closed economy versions of the model, the Phillips curve is defined as a function of the difference between the money supply and the money demand, and the authors explain that in a "two markets economy, excess demand for goods equals excess supply of money".[7] Nobody knows where the capital stock is hidden away, nor why its price does not move to maintain portfolio equilibrium.

In the open versions of the model, domestic prices are a function of the difference between output and desired spending. Although savings were assumed to be a function of the real interest rate, spending is surprisingly made independent of it.[8]

Once the behavior of prices is specified, a case could be made for the existence of credit rationing both in the domestic and foreign markets. Nonetheless, the argument that higher interest rates induce faster growth rates can only be made if savings are found to be a positive function of real interest rates. Empirical evidence in favor of this hypothesis is rather shaky. Fry (1978) reports positive findings for Asian countries. Giovaninni (1982) repeating the very experiment was unable to reject the hypothesis that the elasticity of savings in relation to the interest rate was zero. In Latin America, after the recent disasters with high interest rates in Argentina, Brazil and Chile, few economists will be willing to argue the point that higher interest rates induce faster growth.

---

7. Fry (1982), P. 739 and Kapur (1976).

8. Fry (1982), p. 744 and Mathieson (1980).

6. Structuralism

Discussing definitions and labels is always arbitrary and risky. Table 6 lists beliefs and characteristics commonly attributed to monetarists and structuralists.

TABLE 6

MONETARISTS	STRUCTURALISTS
1. Inflation is bad.	1. Inflation costs are not to be emphasized.
2. The main source of inflation is excess demand due to budget deficits financed by money creation.	2. The main sources of inflation are structural imbalances and rigidities accommodated by passive money.
3. To reduce inflation one must cut domestic credit creation.	3. Costs of reducing inflation are large. Use of incomes policy and price controls are recommended.
4. Monetarists prefer to work with full employment models.	4. Structuralists emphasize unemployment.
5. Monetarist belong to the most conservative groups of society.	5. Structuralists think of themselves as progressive reformists.

The debate between structuralists and monetarists in Latin America has its origins in the debate between industralists and liberals, which started more than a century ago and culminated with the Import Substituting Industrialization (ISI) policies of the postwar period. As opposed to liberals, L.A. industrialists claimed that L.A. had to industrialize to be able to control her economy, breaking a simplistic law of comparative advantage which restricted her to exporting primary goods. Only by creating productive capacity, could she survive slumps in the world economy such as the 1929 crash.

In the fifties, the Economic Commission for Latin America, ECLA, became an important participant in the analysis of the L.A. economy. The strong influence of Hirschman and Raul Prebisch was clear.[9] Prebisch's message was that the world economy had been working to the disadvantage of the primary goods exporters and the way out was to adopt an international commodity agreement and to promote industrialization. Also developed at ECLA was the structuralist interpretation of inflation.

Latin American structuralism claimed that different sectors of the economy develop at different speeds, giving origin to bottlenecks. In the presence of downward price rigidities in some sectors, those bottlenecks originate inflation spurts, that money squeezes cannot correct, although they will most certainly provoke more unemployment. Structuralists thus preached for investment in areas where bottlenecks are supposed to appear (those in which the social revenues exceed the private ones) even if those investments are to be financed by money creation and higher inflation rates.

The structuralist economists have very often been identified as "the money is endogenous" school. The "money is endogenous" statement in the structuralist thought is close to the assumption that monetary authorities accomodate in North American models. It was thus different from endogeneity of money in orthodox models that comes either from the fact that the exchange rate is fixed or from the recognition of the interdependence of monetary and fiscal policies.

Taylor (1981) summarizes the simple short-run structuralist model by the use of three equations:

Equation (1) determines prices from costs (a mark-up equation), with

---

9. See Hirschman (1984) and Prebisch (1984).

components such as wage indexation to incorporate inertial inflation. Equation (2) determines output from aggregate demand. Equation (3) determines assets market equilibrium, with sufficient endogenous variables such as interest rates or money supply to permit (1) and (2) to hold.

Such description makes the structuralist model so close to the recent version of the Keynesian model which incorporates wage contracts, that it is almost impossible to distinguish them. One would have to bring into the analysis other elements besides the algebra, if a distinction was to be made.

Let me take Table 6 into consideration again. Some people who think of themselves as monetarists or structuralists will not agree with some of their listed attributes and will agree with one or two propositions listed under their enemy column. Some, although in strong disagreement with the medicines advocated by their opponents to control inflation, will still understand and learn from their interpretation of the economic world. The fact is that reality has many faces and not all of them are incongruent and exclusive. By now, most monetarists and structuralists in L.A., like monetarists and Keynesians in the North, have agreed that in theory inflation can be induced by both supply and demand shocks, and that its working through the system depends on institutional and structural characteristics of each economy. They diverge quite a bit on speed of adjustments and since so far empirical tests have not been strong enough to reject their different hypothesis, they can stick to their preferred views and policy recommendations. As observed by Dudley Seers (1970), the controversy between monetarists and structuralists "is not just a technical issue in economic theory. At the heart of the controversy are two different ways of looking at economic development, in fact two completely different sets of value judgments about the purposes of economic activity and the ends of economic policy, and two incompatible views on what is politically possible. "

Let us look at one example. Assume one country where half the population is poor and half is rich. The poor want a school. The school can be built under the following alternative set-ups:

(a) Government imposes an income or wealth tax on the rich and uses the revenue to build the school.

(b) Government prints money and finances the construction of the school through the inflation that falls on both groups.

(c) Government stays out, on the argument that if the poor really wanted a school, they would find a way of building it while the rich can pay the police to protect their property.

It is clear that under (a) there is no reason to assume that inflation is around the corner, while in (b) it is very clear where it came from. Egalitarian people would argue in favor of (a). Structuralists might argue that, if the wealth tax cannot be imposed, one should still have resource to (b) and live with inflation. Monetarists might identify with the last position.

Sometimes the origin of inflation is not as easy to identify as in the example above. Not only because its origin gets blurred by many intervening factors, but also because inflationary finance is not the unique source of inflation. And here a structuralist would call our attention to two different sources of rigidities: one resulting from the different development paths of different sectors of the economy and other resulting from the struggle of different groups in society to protect their share in income.

The Taylor model described above can be extended from one to several sectors to emphasize the structuralist interpretation where changes in relative prices of different outputs can play a role in the adjustment process. The story runs as follows. During the process of industrialization there is a shift of resources from the agricultural to the industrial sector. With a stagnant food producing sector, growth in the industrial sector will increase the demand for food while reducing its supply. Because of the inadequacy of the purchasing power of exports which prevents sufficient food imports, excess demand for food induces increasing prices. Yet those price increases are not matched by price declines in the industrial sector in response to excess supply, where prices are marked-up over wages, whose behavior depends on the behavior of food prices. Hence overall inflation is induced and ratified by monetary policy in order to maintain employment.[10]

Wachter (1976) modifies the rigidity of supply in the agricultural sector assuming that prices may adjust symmetrically but with different speed in both sectors. If food prices react more quickly than other prices, a price increase for food due to excess demand cannot be matched by a decline of price of another product in the same period.

Structuralists would still insist that the inflation process cannot be fully understood by appeal just to budget deficits, cyclical unemployment and bottlenecks. Behind it also lies the struggle of different groups in society trying to get a larger piece of the cake. The models developed in sections 2 and 3 assumed a constant mark-up. A process of adjustment through reduced real wages and expansion of

---

10. A formalization of this model is found in Cardoso (1981).

employment in the export sector puts its burden entirely on wage earners. Structuralists would argue that prices control during the adjustment process will help distribute the costs of adjustment and avoid income distribution deterioration, so often associated with stabilization programs. There is no magic exchange rate or cut in budget deficits that will solve the problems of inequality.

Skidmore and Smith (1984) note that the Prebisch-ECLA-Structuralist analysis furnished ammunition for centrist politicians such as Vargas and Kubitscheck in Brazil, Frondizi in Argentina and Frei in Chile. It is more difficult to find examples of its use as a stabilization machine, but price controls and income policy have been present in many programs, like the 1965/67 experiment in Brazil. In 1985, Alfonsin in Argentina, Sarney in Brazil and Garcia Perez in Peru started to resist the IMF conditionality programs, claiming that either growth is restored in L.A. or democracy is condemned in their countries. They propose a recovery of their economies and the use of incomes policy. Their success will depend on how far they can carry needed reforms and the sectoral programs that are at the heart of the structuralist propositions, before the pressures of workers for wage readjustments make both the external imbalance and the inflation rate intolerable.

REFERENCES

_ Cardoso, Eliana (1981), "Food Supply and Inflation", Journal of Development Economics, pp. 269-84.

- Cooper, Richard (1971), Currency Devaluations in Developing Countries, Princeton Essays in International Finance, no. 86.

_ Cline, William (1981), "Economic Stabilization in Peru, 1975-78" in Cline and Weintraub, eds., Economic Stabilization in Developing Countries, The Brookings Institution.

_ Diaz-Alejandro, Carlos (1981), "Southern Cone Stabilization Policies", in Cline and Weintraub, eds., opus cit.

_____ (1983), "Stories of the 1930's to the 1980's", in Aspe and Dornbusch, eds., Financial Policies and the World Capital Market: The Problem of Latin American Countries, Chicago: The University of Chicago Press.

_ Dornbusch, Rudiger (1981), Open Economy Macroeconomics, Basic Books.

_____ (1982), "Stabilization Policies in Developing Countries: What Have We Learned?," World Development, 10(9), pp. 701-8.

_____ (1984), "External Debt, Budget Deficits and Disequilibrium Exchange Rates", in Smith and Cuddington, eds., International Debt and the Developing Countries, Washington: The World Bank.

_ Fishlow, Albert (1975), "Some Reflections on Post-64 Brazilian Economic Policy", in Stepan, ed., Authoritarian Brazil, Yale University Press.

_ Foxley, Alejandro (1981), "Stabilization Policies and their Effects on Employment and Income Distribution: A Latin American Perspective", in Cline and Weintraub, eds., Economic Stabilization in Developing Countries, The Brookings Institution.

_ Fry, Maxwell (1978), "Money and Capital or Financial Deepening in Economic Development?", Journal of Money, Credit and Banking, 10(4), pp. 464-75.

_____ (1982), "Models of Financially Repressed Developing Economies," World Development, 10(9), pp. 731-50.

_ Giovaninni, Alberto (1982), "The Interest Elasticity of Savings in Developing Countries: The Existing Evidence," MIT: Mimeo.

_ Hirschman, Albert O., "A Dissenter's Confession: The Strategy of Economic Development Revisited", in Meier and Seers, eds., Pioneers in Development, Oxford: The Oxford University Press.

_ Harberger, Arnold (1982), "The Chilean Economy in the 1970's: Crisis, Stabilization, Liberalization, Reform," Carnegie-Rochester Conference Series on Public Policy, vol. 17, pp. 115-52.

_ Kapur, Basant (1976), "Alternative Stabilization Policies for Less Developed Economics," Journal of Political Economy, 84(4), pp. 777-95.

_ Macedo, Roberto (1977), "A Critical Review of the Relation Between Post-65 Wage Policy and the Worsening of Brazil's Size Income Distribution in the 1960's," Explorations in Economic Research, 4(1), pp. 117-40.

_ Mathieson, Donald (1979), "Financial Reform and Capital Flows in a Developing Economy," IMF Staff Papers, 26(3), pp. 450-89.

_ MacKinnon, Ronald (1973), Money and Capital in Economic Development, The Brookings Institution.

_ Meade, James (1951), The Balance of Payments, Oxford University Press.

_ Mundell, Robert (1968), International Economics, MacMillan.

_ Prebisch, Raul (1984), "Five Stages in My Thinking on Development," in Meier and Seer, eds., Pioneers in Development, Oxford: Oxford University Press.

_ Ramos, Joseph (1980), "The Economics of Hyperstagflation: Stabilization Policy in Post-1973 Chile," Journal of Development Economics, 7(4), pp. 467-88.

_ Rodriguez, Carlos Alfredo (1982), "The Argentine Stabilization Plan of December 20th," World Development, 10(9), pp. 801-12.

_ Skidmore, Thomas and Peter Smith (1984), Modern Latin America, Oxford: Oxford University Press.

_ Taylor, Lance (1981), Structuralist Macroeconomics, New York: Basic Books.

_ Thorp, Rosemary and G. Bertram (1978), Peru: 1880-1977: Growth and Policy in an Open Economy, New York: Columbia University Press.

_____ (1984), Latin America in the 1930's, Oxford: MacMillan in association with St. Antony's College.

_ Watcher, Susan (1976), Latin American Inflation, Lexington: D.C. Heath and Co.

_ Weintraub, Sidney (1981), "Case Study of Economic Stabilization: Mexico," in Cline and Weintraub, eds., Economic Stabilization in Developing Countries, The Brookings Institution.

_ Williamson, John (1982) "A Comparison of Macroeconomic Strategies in South America," Institute for International Economics: Mimeo.

DATE DUE

MAY 0 5 1995

DATE DUE

MAY 0 6 1992			
DEC 2 2 1995			
DEC 0 5 2000			

Demco, Inc. 38-293